RESCUING MORGAN

LOVE IS JUST THE BEGINNING

DAN PERDIOS

Paperback ISBN: 979-8-35091-305-7

eBook ISBN: 979-8-35091-306-4

Printed in the United States of America

For all those who open their
hearts and homes to rescue animals

CHAPTER ONE

A DOG-LESS HOME

WE BOARDED THE PLANE IN PALM SPRINGS ON A HOT, sweltering, July morning. It was 2008 and this was my first trip to Cape Cod in twenty-five years without a Golden Retriever at my side. In Dallas, where we had a layover, James and I said goodbye to each other. James, my partner of five years, was traveling to Baltimore to see his parents. As we embraced, he said, "Take care of yourself. Call me if you need to." He was concerned about my well-being while staying with my family, as was I.

The flight to Logan in Boston was three and a half hours long. Most of what I remember was just staring at the seat in front of me, my heart fractured. I had planned the visit assuming my Golden boy, Willy, would have accompanied me. He always liked flying. The other passengers and flight attendants showered him with lots of attention.

One time on our way "Back East" the attendants let him up on the seat, brought him blankets and pillows, and even a meal. They pulled out their phones and showed me photographs of their pets. Since 9/11, this would never happen.

You might be wondering how I was able to bring my dog right on board. Surely, mobility wasn't a problem for me. I wasn't in a wheelchair. Nor was vision an issue. However, during the worst of the AIDS pandemic, I experienced chronic sinus and ear infections causing my eardrums to burst. This sounds painful, and it was. When these infections flared up, I was made completely deaf. Weeks went by before the antibiotics kicked in. The bouts happened so frequently my eardrums never closed over. So I was forced to wear hearing aids starting in 1990. Fortunately, the San Francisco Bay Area Hearing Society loaned me a pair. Even so, my ear doctor advised me to keep them out whenever I could. Back in those days, people with AIDS contracted some seriously strange illnesses and my ENT (ear, nose and throat) specialist didn't want an infection going into my brain.

In 1998 Willy became my legally licensed service dog for my hearing. He alerted me to people and animals; knocks on the door. Patrolling the area around me. Especially in the evening when it was dark. Once he saved my house from burning down when I didn't hear the smoke alarm. Willy entered the bedroom and stared at me until I finally got up. He led me into the kitchen where I found the stove on fire.

Willy gets the credit for introducing James and me to each other one spring day at the local coffee shop, Koffi. He had free-range of the large grassy courtyard behind the cafe. He started begging at James' table. So much so, that he even pawed to get some food. I had to get up and retrieve my retriever. That's how James and I met. Just like in "101 Dalmatians," when Pango wants to meet Perdita, and the owners meet, too.

The first morning home at my parents' beach house, I sat with my mother in the enclosed summer porch room. As I sipped Irish Breakfast tea, she said, "It's strange for you to be home without a dog."

"Feels really strange to me, too."

My mother was a small, slender, but still beautiful woman, who continued to smoke too much. While I'm around she pretended she didn't smoke in the house. Then I'd catch her walking through the kitchen with a lit cigarette, and the pretension ended.

"You look tired. And you've lost some weight."

"Well, we've gotten that out of the way," I replied. My mother reminds me of Doris Roberts in *Everybody Loves Raymond*. Or should I say Doris Roberts is based on my mother since she'd been doing it a lot longer than that show.

Such comments about my appearance used to bother me and send me into a tailspin. I'd be concerned now if she *didn't* say those things. I always hoped to come home and hear her say, "You look good." By now, after so many years of living away I realize those words will never be spoken and maybe they were never supposed to.

The fact is when I moved to Palm Springs in 2003, I hired a trainer to help me with my workouts, solely to gain weight. I now weighed ten pounds more since I last saw her. More than I ever had. I was a bulging one hundred and eighty-five pounds. For my height of five feet ten inches, I was a buffed machine and I never looked better.

Then she asked, "When will you get another one?"

"Not sure." I shrugged. "When I get back." I gazed out the window observing what had changed and what had remained the same over the last year in the green woods surrounding their house. I loved how their place looked out over the trees. I noticed a large branch of the old Oak tree lying on the ground. Some windy storm must have taken it down.

She was right. Being there alone was strange. Three months had gone by since Willy's passing. I missed him terribly. His congestive heart illness took him so quickly. One day we were hiking up a steep mountain. Within a week he could barely breathe. I blamed myself for not getting him to the vet more quickly. Perhaps he'd be here with me if I had.

I settled back in the thick-cushioned wicker chair and exhaled. "I'm probably going to rescue a dog," I answered. I shared with her about all the animals turned in to shelters because of the rash of recent foreclosures. "I already signed up online with a few different groups who rescued Goldens." She was pleased with the idea. She knew how important a dog was in my life.

My parents' house sits on a knoll above Lake Elizabeth and Red Lily Pond on Cape Cod. These two small lakes are situated between their house and Craigville Beach, four blocks away. In the past, Willy and I rose each morning at the crack of dawn, sometimes beating sunrise. We strolled down the road by the lakes, pausing to search for the two white swans that resided here year-round. They're so majestic. I felt lucky to see these magical animals. The same feeling you would get, I imagine, if you saw a white unicorn.

From the lake our adventure would ramble along the edge of the Craigville Retreat Center. This religious organization believes that "No matter who – no matter what - no matter where we are on life's journey – notwithstanding race, gender identity or expression, sexual orientation, class or creed – we all belong to God and to one worldwide community of faith." Often we saw bumper stickers with pro-environment messages and even rainbow flags and equality stickers.

A Golden Retriever named Abigail had lived at the house on one corner, where the lake and the complex bordered. Abi would push the screen door open, dash out to us, barking and hopping. She and Willy scooted in and out of the lake. Then one summer the house was quiet. As I walked by the property on this dog-less summer morning, my heart ached. The loneliness was heavy on my shoulders. These sweet creatures never live long enough.

Dogs are allowed on Craigville Beach from September 15 through May 15. Though it's no secret that dog owners use the beach year-round. The catch was to go before the college kids who staffed the entrance booth arrived and before the police finished their coffee and Boston creams at Dunkin Donuts.

Getting up so early was worth the effort to have the beach to ourselves. Occasionally, a lone fisherman, or a swimmer, would be the only other human presence. By 9 a.m. the beach would be packed with people. Not something I took pleasure in. Rules are strictly enforced at Craigville Beach. The regulation sign is huge, prominent, and expansive. Resident parking permits are required year-round. No smoking. No alcohol. No obscenities toward employees. Swim in designated areas only. Flotation devices only if there's an onshore breeze. All umbrellas must be secured properly and not obstruct the lifeguard. No breach of peace. Drones are prohibited. No dogs. All in all, there are fifteen posted rules. Apparently nudity is allowed. (Just kidding.) Actually, I agree with each and every one of these rules except of course, the canine rule. But even this rule is one I support in the heat of the summer. No dog ought to be on a hot crowded beach where their paws might burn.

Each morning, walking along Craigville Beach, I felt Willy with me. I could see him splashing through the water and diving above the waves. As I rested in our favorite spot, out on the breakers protecting the marsh, where we watched the gulls and terns glide by and the surf split in two, I felt him sitting next to me and licking my cheeks. A memory comforting and lonely at the same time. Tears streamed down my face.

These excursions "Back East" were never without problems. My relationship with my parents was always rocky. But since the Cape Cod house wasn't the home from my youth, the button pushing wasn't as strong. No matter what, my father always managed to find something to criticize me about. I'm not exaggerating. On a previous visit, I questioned him why he picked on me so often and he replied, "Cause you're such an easy target." My father was always a bully to me. When I was eighteen, and told him I was gay, he dragged me down the stairs and beat me. As a result, I tried to avoid him as much as I could. Having Willy with me always made these moments more bearable. He was my release valve. My escape. I could easily grab the leash and get out the door to avoid my father's verbal assaults.

In March 2008, Willy crossed over. March became April and not only was there no dog, there was also no plan to get one either. The solution was simple enough; people got pets all the time. You buy a dog from a breeder or you rescue one from a shelter. Obviously my emotions and my brain were so scrambled nothing seemed clear. One day I wanted a puppy. The next day I wasn't sure. Maybe a slightly older dog would be better. One day I felt ready. The next day the thought of replacing Willy sent me into despair and I realized it was still too soon.

If you've never had a dog, you might not understand how I felt. There was no heavier silence than waking up at night and not hearing Willy snoring on the floor next to the bed. No more click-clack of his nails on the cement patio. Even after a month, I continued to automatically save a few bites of food from my plate for him. The moment the loss really hit home, I was walking downtown and saw my reflection in a store window. Willy wasn't there.

For me, personally, grief has had such a profound impact on my life. Beginning with the assassination of my gay rights hero, Harvey Milk, and San Francisco Mayor George Moscone in 1978. I joined thirty thousand mourners in a candlelight march down Market Street to City Hall. I knew Harvey Milk. He was a regular customer at the restaurant where I worked and we'd talk. He'd ask me how school was going and if I had heard from my parents. Just as he had become a national leader, he was gone. This was a collective kind of grief.

Three short years later, in 1981, AIDS ripped through the San Francisco gay community. Many of my friends were wasting and dying. These losses were more personal. My then-partner, Rick, the man I wanted to spend my life with, died of AIDS in 1987. We were so young. I was only twenty-nine. He was thirty-eight. Rick was the best thing that had ever happened to me. Meeting him changed my life for the better. He was the first of my close friends to succumb to the disease. Although not the last. For the next ten years so many of my friends and acquaintances got sick and perished I ceased counting. And always, the prospect of my own impending illness and demise haunted me.

In a recent *Wall Street Journal* article about the impact of COVID deaths, the opening sentence states "the disease is also unraveling families and communities in subtler ways... It robbed society of grandparents, parents, spouses, sons and daughters, best friends, mentors, loyal employees, and bosses.... It's catastrophic...an enormous loss of life."

I know first-hand how this feels, how this affects individuals. My life with Rick in our Castro Street neighborhood was where my dreams and my hopes laid. My safe harbor. My optimism. My happiness.

I'm pleased to see how the *Wall Street Journal* has expanded grief to include "best friends, bosses, employees, mentors." I'm grateful these relationships have been acknowledged, validated, and honored. Our grief during the AIDS epidemic was never acknowledged. Never validated. Never honored.

Grief is such an intimate experience. There is no right or wrong way to process these deep, conflicting emotions. Many of us believe our dogs are family. So losing your dog was losing a loved one. Willy's crossing over brought up so much old grief, an old sadness. Feelings I believed I had handled came roaring back and they overwhelmed me.

Like the day I arrived at the hospital and they were taking Rick downstairs to put a catheter in his heart. The doctors told us it was the right thing to do. I didn't really understand what they were doing or why they were doing it. The procedure seemed so final. So fatal. But Rick had made the decision.

The elevator ride down was the first time I cried in front of Rick. He told me to stop but I couldn't. I was too tired, too broken. The elevator doors opened and ahead of us were two wooden doors, with a sign that read: NO ADMITTANCE. I could barely breathe. They took Rick through those doors. I wasn't allowed to follow them. After the doors closed, I stood in the hallway. Alone. I sank to the floor against a wall and put my head between my knees and cried. I don't know how long I sat there. When I looked up, I didn't know what to do, where I was, or where to go. All I knew was that Rick was gone.

And now, with Willy gone, I was having those same feelings. When you lose someone, you just don't know whether you can go on without them. But you find a way to go on. Sometimes the only thing I could do was go to bed. I took comfort in a quote I found from Winnie the Pooh. *"If there ever comes a day where we can't be together, keep me in your heart. I'll stay there forever."*

By Memorial Day, three months post Willy's death, the loneliness had grown so painful I could no longer bear it. The news was full of stories about thousands of people losing their homes because of the "Great Recession" and abandoning their pets. Golden Retrievers included. With James in my life and my health stable, I decided to forgo having a trained hearing dog for the time being. I had to do something for these poor animals with no home.

So I began my search for a Golden to rescue. Golden Retrievers had done so much for me. They rescued me. They saved my life. This was an opportunity for me to thank them and pay them back. My first dog, Nicholas, was a Golden. He was my loyal friend during the worst of the AIDS epidemic. I truly believe that if I hadn't had Nicholas in my life I would have succumbed to the disease. Then there was Willy who helped me to climb out of the depression that engulfed me before the newer HIV meds began to work. His extroverted personality forced me out of the house. The sunshine of his smile brightened my life, and with his joyful spirit for living we were able to move to Palm Springs and start life over again. I never could have accomplished this move without Willy by my side.

Friends told me about several websites for adoption organizations. The Golden Retriever Rescue in Los Angeles had the most dogs, over forty. My heart broke each time I saw all the Goldens needing a home. Some of the older dogs with white faces made me cry and my grief roared up. James counseled me to limit the amount of time on their website for my own emotional well-being.

He was right. I wanted to rescue all of them. Naturally, that was impossible. Nevertheless, one particular dog grabbed my attention. His name was Sparky, a one-year-old pup. The first thing you noticed was the long red tongue sticking out the side of his mouth, dangling far below. He had those big droopy ears hanging from his small broad head, which typified the breed. His nose was as dark as coal at the tip of his snout. His thin black lips looked as if they had been penciled in. Though his picture was adorable at first glance, Sparky didn't look happy. His name might have been Sparky, but he didn't sparkle. His lips didn't form a smile. His face was skinny, and you could see indentations beneath his eyes and around his nose. The fur along his body was ruffled and bulky yet you could see his ribs sticking out. Sparky was the one I aspired to help.

I was excited to go to their website to let them know I wished to adopt Sparky. I thought the process would be easy. My first two Goldens had been from small local breeders. I had friends who went to a shelter and within a day had a new pet. Imagine my surprise to discover their application required answers to over forty questions, as comprehensive as applying for a job. They needed to know every detail of how their "rescue" would be cared for. Certainly, questions such as how much exercise I would give my dog and how big my yard was made sense to me. Unexpectedly, one question asked, "What would you do if your new dog chewed your belongings or showed other destructive behavior?" I'd already been through the first part of this question. Every puppy chews things. But then the second half was confusing. What kind of destructive behavior could a Golden Retriever have? Another question asked what issues I was willing to work on with a new dog? What issues were they talking about? I was sure there was nothing I couldn't handle as an experienced dog owner. They are the most easy-going and loving dogs around. How little did I know!

I wondered how many days would go by before I heard back from them. Even though I was a Golden companion for over twenty-five years, I was still nervous whether I had answered their questions correctly. I must have met their requirements because in two days a local Palm Springs volunteer called me to make an appointment to see the house. The short turnaround both startled and impressed me. I was positive I would surpass any inspection with flying colors.

At the agreed time an older soft-spoken gentleman from the LA Retriever group arrived at my house. As we walked the property, he informed me I needed to make some changes to the yard, such as removing my crown of thorns. He pointed out the Japanese oleander and said they were poisonous to dogs. I didn't even know the shrub was an oleander. The plant was there when I bought the house. He also stipulated to fence off areas around my favorite specimen of an ocotillo, with its long spiny stalks. The name means "little torch" in Spanish for the orange flaming appearance of the blooms. I was shocked and then miffed. His suggestions were upsetting. I thought he just needed to see the dog wouldn't be going to some crack house or junkyard, and to see if the property was securely fenced in. I never expected him to tell me to make changes to my landscaping. When I told him my last dog didn't have any problems with these plants, he replied the new rescue wasn't going to know to stay out of these beds and could hurt himself.

By afternoon on that day, I had accepted he was right. I had forgotten when Willy was a puppy he romped around all of my flowerbeds until I fenced them off. In that case, the safeguard had been for my plants' protection, not his. This time the barrier would be for both the plants and the dog. I was determined whatever hoops they threw at me I would jump through. I could easily drive over to Lowe's or Home Depot and wrap plastic orange fencing around these plants.

While the rescue volunteer checked my house, I casually mentioned to him we were leaving in a week for the East Coast. He stiffened and alerted me I'd have to wait until returning to adopt. This news was perplexing and I questioned why they couldn't hold Sparky until I got back. He explained their policy was to not hold dogs, since people often changed their minds. When I protested I wasn't going to change my mind, he just shook his head.

Upset, I immediately phoned James and informed him they wouldn't hold Sparky for us while we were away. He tried to calm me. He was confident Sparky would be available when we got back. I shook my head, I knew better. Someone would scoop a young Golden up fast.

In a calmer moment, I recognized this policy was for the animal's best interest. Some people do change their minds and the dog was the one who remained homeless. I had never adopted a dog before, and this process was all so new to me. My emotions were ricocheting off the walls and I wasn't thinking coherently.

Soon I would miss the beauty of Cape Cod, but I was eager to return home to California to resume the search for our new best friend. Each day I scanned the adoption sites, Sparky's profile was still there.

Back in Palm Springs, despite the fact he was still visible online as obtainable, the woman from the rescue group said he wasn't. Such a disappointment. I had hoped Sparky would be coming home to live with us, and I really thought the rescue was meant to be. Sadly, I refocused my attention elsewhere.

Finally, we drove to see a dog in Orange County, two hours away. His name was Alex, about a year old. We liked his age and his reddish color. Getting another blond one would only remind me of Willy.

Right away, we saw Alex didn't have a bushy Golden tail. What I loved about Willy's tail was that it curved straight up into the sky, swaying back and forth. His long feathering fur fluttered like a flag in the breeze on the Fourth of July. This tail appeared narrower, not fluffy, more like a German Shepherd's.

This mixed breed was nice, but we just didn't fall in love. I wanted a Golden Retriever. I'm a Golden guy. Goldens have a unique quality to them. They're one of the slowest maturing dogs. Puppy stage can last until four or five. During this time they need, no *demand*, constant attention. At the end of this growth, they become so keyed into their human owners they act as though they can read our thoughts and finish our sentences. They heal people. That's why they're used in hospitals to visit patients. A Golden Retriever opens your heart.

Alex would never be a Golden. I would forever be comparing him to Willy. I'm glad James was there. I felt so sad saying no. I cried in the car when we left, leaving this poor baby behind. If I were alone, I probably would have taken him.

Elena, the woman from the rescue group, scolded me, "You see a dog with the intent to adopt," her email read. "What was wrong with this dog?"

"It wasn't a match," I wrote back. "He wasn't a Golden Retriever."

"You're doing this for the dog," her email growled. "We don't take physical appearance into consideration when we match dogs. Ninety-five percent of people who see a dog adopt."

"I'm sorry. Of course, you are right. But it just wasn't a match for me," I responded. I had to follow my gut. And yes, I am doing this for the dog, but the adoption most definitely has to be a match. Why would she want people to take an animal that wasn't a perfect fit? I really had some doubts about this organization if this is how they treated people.

Fresh from the painful experience with the dog in Orange County I didn't know what to do. Over the next two weeks, I kept asking about dogs, each time Elana said there were no matches for me. Now I really felt as if I was being punished. I worried the longer I went without a dog the greater the likelihood of never getting another one grew. The last six months seemed like six years. What if James decided he preferred not having a dog? What would I do then? I considered going to one of the public shelters myself, before the rescue people got there, so they couldn't shut me out. But there were so many shelters and where would I begin?

James had more patience than I did. He was better at waiting for things. He was a film producer. In his business of filmmaking, deals rarely went as planned and he always had to adjust. He soon tired of listening to my disappointment and feelings of loneliness. Sparky's picture was still posted on their website, so James sent Elena, the woman from the rescue organization, an email. "We're going to be in Los Angeles on the weekend of August 16. We'd like to see Sparky."

In the afternoon, a message came: "One of our volunteers can introduce you to Sparky on Saturday morning, August 16, at the Culver City Veterinarian office at 10:30 a.m., provided you go with the intention to adopt."

In other words, bring your checkbook.

CHAPTER TWO

THE RESCUE

ON THE MORNING WE WERE SUPPOSED TO PICK up Sparky I woke with an uneasy pain in my stomach. I didn't trust the rescue was going to happen. I was fearful if we showed up late, they would refuse to give us the dog. I worried they'd find some reason not to let us have Sparky. I insisted we leave early. We rushed out of our apartment in West Hollywood for the ten-mile drive to Culver City. It's a good thing we did because in our excitement we got lost. By the time we arrived at the appointment, my nerves were frayed. To my relief, we drove up exactly at ten thirty.

A young fair-haired woman in blue denim shorts swiftly led a small Golden out to us in the parking lot. She introduced herself as Donna, then waved her hand downward and announced this was Sparky. Just as I mentioned how adorable he was, he sprang up and caught my arm with his mouth. His clamp was startlingly strong, and his sharp teeth dug into my skin and were hurtful. He didn't let go easily. Rescuing my arm from Sparky's clutches required some twisting and cajoling.

Without any attempt to control him, Donna calmly told me, "He does that." Her casual manner and lack of apology were surprising to me, more so than the dog's clench of my arm. This time I knelt down so he wouldn't pounce again and said hello to Sparky. This could be my next dog. The meeting was as close to love at first sight as possible. He noticeably had gained a little weight since the photo, though his ribs protruded. I extended my hand along his back and felt the bones of his spine and cringed. He was small for a one-year-old male. For Goldens, big is not necessarily better; the size can be more difficult on their hind legs and harder on the owner's back when you have to lift them in their older years. I learned this from personal experience with my first Golden, Nicholas. We had lived on a hill and I had to carry him up steep steps to the street when he became a senior.

Donna relinquished Sparky's leash to me and led us over to her SUV. When she opened the rear hatch Sparky immediately vaulted in. There were milk crates filled with bags of dog food and toys, with a briefcase next to them. She counseled us, "Sparky eats too fast." Then recommended, "When you feed him . . ." She paused in mid-sentence and rubbed Sparky's head, then proceeded, "Try putting a ball in his bowl to slow him down a bit." There was a hint of sadness in her voice as she urged us to go first when we exited the house. "You should make him sit and wait until you are out the door," she advised. "He needs to learn this." The tenderness in her instructions for Sparky made me realize how hard giving him away was for her. I could empathize. I would have difficulty as well. I'd make a lousy foster dad.

Then another car steered into the lot. There was a sugar-faced Golden in the back seat. His fur had grown white around his eyes and nose. I was familiar with this look. Sparky dove out of the SUV and thrust forward towards the car, barking aggressively. Clumsily, I seized the leash, somewhat stunned, and hauled him back close to me. For a small dog he sure was strong.

Again, without any attempt to correct him, Donna offhandedly cautioned us Sparky had trouble with other dogs. When I eyed James, the smile on his face was gone and he wanted to know Sparky's story. We learned he had been rescued from a shelter in South LA. His owner had surrendered him for biting. That's all the rescue group knew. Sparky had been in rough shape when they got him. She said with some basic training and lots of love he'd be a great pet.

This interaction was worrisome, and I could tell by his scowl James wasn't yet on board with Sparky. But her statement resonated with me. I'm a love-will-conquer-all kind of guy. With enough love, Sparky would be friendly; with enough positive reinforcement he'd behave. I honestly believed this. I also figured this might be our one and only chance for a dog. I didn't know how much longer I could endure this topsy-turvy emotional rollercoaster. We had been forewarned to come intending to adopt. How would the woman from the rescue group react to another unsuccessful meet and greet?

Our ride home was slow and cautious so as not to upset the new passenger sitting behind us. I couldn't resist turning around and repeating, "He's our boy! He's our boy!"

Outside our apartment building Sparky halted and was reluctant to go up the two cement steps to the first landing. He lingered on the sidewalk and actually recoiled from the staircase. His behavior confounded me, and I pleaded with him to try. He simply refused to budge.

James stood next to the foyer door propping it ajar. "What's wrong with him?" he asked, peering over the railing at me. "Does he not know how to go up stairs?"

"I don't know. He seems afraid to even come near them," I replied. Sparky wasn't even curious. What young dog can't go up two steps? No matter how much I coaxed him it was futile. I had never encountered this problem before. I slipped my arms underneath him and lifted Sparky up to the wide landing, then abruptly rotated around and hurtled back down to make a game out of the situation in hopes of exciting him to overcome his reluctance, but he rebuffed my effort.

Sparky and I stared at each other. I wondered what he might be thinking. Was he scared? Nervous? Happy? He looked so cute. I couldn't refrain from angling toward him, game-like. We still had a stalemate.

To speed things along I scooped him up and carried him to the entrance level. Here, he excitedly ran past the opened glass security doors into the atrium, then suddenly froze again at the narrow stairwell leading up to our second-floor apartment.

Neither of us had any idea what his aversion might be since no one had warned us. Why didn't anyone tell us about this? How could they not have known? I patted the stairs in hopes of encouraging him. Frustratingly, whatever I tried proved to be a dead end. I suppose it was possible the rescue group didn't know about his trepidation. Something must have happened because a young dog was usually inquisitive about everything. Sparky seemed apprehensive to even come near them. Now the task was left to us to help him overcome his fear.

Since we were making no progress, I lugged him up the remaining thirteen steps. His papers said he only weighed fifty-five pounds. Some Goldens that age can weigh nearly sixty-five pounds or more. But those were just numbers in my head. Only after I raised him and felt his rib cage did I fully comprehend what Sparky must have suffered.

After I lowered him down gently, Sparky raced into the master bedroom and back out. He hurried into the bathroom and out. We noted him sniffing each and every corner and we assumed he could still smell Willy after five months. James asked whether we were going to keep his name. I replied no and shared the story about Kermit, one of my neighbors at the Russian River. He had a Dalmatian named Sparky, who was always escaping. There wasn't a day I didn't hear

Kermit shouting from his deck in his Guatemalan accent, "Spar-kay, Spar-kay!" It always made me laugh because he sounded exactly like the Latino houseboy in the movie, *The Birdcage*.

James suggested Russell. We both repeated the name a couple of times and decided it was much too "button-down" for Sparky. We tossed about a few other names and tried them out, but they didn't fit. Then I posed Morgan, after the spiced rum pirate, Captain Morgan. We both laughed and in unison exclaimed, "That's it!"

James called out his name and of course Morgan didn't respond. He dashed into James' office and scampered out triumphantly with a sock dangling from his mouth. When we tried to take the prize, he skedaddled away. We cornered him and played tug-of-war. The sock was a good one, so we didn't want him to tear a hole in it. He didn't give up the treasure freely. James finally pried open his mouth and jerked it out. The evidence was clear: Morgan needed toys, so we headed off to Petco.

Getting Morgan down the stairs proved much simpler than going up. I knew gravity would be our ally. To get off the landing, I stationed his two front paws on the lower first step, then helped him down to the next one. From here, he slid down a few more and finally was on his way. At the bottom he galloped out the entrance door, blew past the outside stairs like a pro, down to the street. After this, Morgan's bathmophobia miraculously disappeared permanently. It was so strange, yet such a relief.

Morgan yanked on his leash, physically dragging me, as we made our way along Santa Monica Boulevard. I couldn't believe how strong he was. I glanced at James and he was shaking his head in dismay. After several years together, you knew what certain gestures meant. James preferred things calm and slow, without surprises. At the corner we crossed to the other side and strode along the tree-lined parkway into Beverly Hills at a fast pace, as Morgan strained onward. Ultimately, my arm got tired from the battle, and I implored James to take him for a while. He too was amazed at how energetic and powerful Morgan was as he tried to restrain him from blasting down the path. When people with a Boxer came from the opposite direction James handed the leash to me.

I admit, I was ill at ease about the possibility of a contentious confrontation with the approaching dog. I grasped the leash firmly and we stood aside to let them pass. Morgan crouched and without any warning sprung towards the large dog, barking ferociously. "No," I shouted, jolting the leash to bring him back. "Morgan, sit." Morgan didn't respond to my commands. He continued to snarl and lunged towards the well-built canine. I gripped the leash with both hands to keep them from getting close. The unsuspecting owners and their Boxer seemed startled by this exchange.

"Sorry. He's a rescue. We just got him," I said.

As they walked farther down the pathway, Morgan finally stopped growling. His breathing was heavy, and his chest heaved in and out. James glared at me and uttered, "This cannot happen every time we walk by a dog."

"I agree. I don't like it either..." I sensed he was judging me. As though I had done something wrong. "You're being unreasonable. It isn't going to change instantly. We just got him. For God's sake." I marched Morgan forward. Away from James. As we walked ahead, I wondered how we were going to change Morgan's aggression. I had never experienced anything similar to this before. Willy was the friendliest dog around. I never had to worry. Didn't matter whom he interacted with: Pit Bulls, Shepherds, Dobermans, Rottweilers, or Boxers. Willy romped with them all. I loved to witness when another dog ran up to him to cause trouble. Willy just rolled over in a submissive manner. And that was that. The aggressor would stand there, unsure what to do. Then the two of them zoomed off horseplaying together. At first, I thought his passive behavior was a fluke thing. But after a while I definitely saw a pattern. Willy had no interest in fighting.

Only once, at the park, was there ever trouble when another dog continued to hump Willy and wouldn't give up. At first, I found the encounter amusing and assumed they'd work the issue out. When the alpha behavior didn't stop, I could see Willy start to get irritated. He was almost twelve then and I worried about his legs. I felt I had to protect him. The owner was on his cell phone, nearby, ignoring the problem. I asked him twice to take care of his Chow. Rudely, he pivoted away from me. At the same time, Willy had had enough and twisted towards the humper and a fight ensued. Well, I had had enough as well and grabbed the animal's collar and flung him off Willy. Boy, this sure got the guy's attention! Then he tried to tell me I was at fault. I wasn't buying his accusation. I persisted, "Get off your phone and control your dog. Keep him away from us." Now, here we were with Morgan. The uncontrollable one. How was I going to fix this, I wondered as we walked farther along?

When we arrived at the Beverly Hills Petco, we were surprised to see the parking lot stacked with cages of dogs and cats of all sizes and ages available for adoption. The set up was sad to see. So many animals needing homes reminded us of why we had Morgan. To avoid any incident, we kept him moving. He towed us right inside.

The first thing necessary was an identification tag for his collar. One with both the city and desert address etched on the ID. Afterwards, I proposed we try a harness to help hold him back. I'd seen a lot of people use them and thought we should try one. James told me to get whatever I needed since I was the one who was going to train him. Although he was both of ours, with James now teaching screenwriting at the University of Southern California, Morgan was going to be my responsibility. I'm the one he'd be with, day in and day out, and I was fine with that. Too many cooks in the kitchen kind of thing. I knew if a problem came up, I could count on James to step forward, as he did when Willy became ill.

We maintained a safe distance from other shop patrons as we wandered around the store, checking each aisle to see if it was dog-occupied before we advanced. All the employees crowded around to meet him and asked if they could give him treats. Customers wished to say hello and to pet our new boy. James joked Morgan had "moved on up" from South Central LA to Beverly Hills in one day. Every indication showed Morgan was going to attract lots of admirers just like Willy did, as Goldens always do. Only with Morgan, he was going to need lots of supervision before I could trust him around any dogs or people.

When we climbed into bed that night, Morgan soared up onto the mattress and just as suddenly spun and leapt off. He sped out into the living room and sprinted back into the bedroom, hurtling up onto the bed again and then shot off like a cannon ball around the apartment.

In a bewildered tone, James asked, "What's he doing?"

I didn't have a clue. "Playing, I think," I responded, as Morgan whirled through the apartment, again and again. I felt like I was watching a "Road Runner" cartoon. I expected to hear "Beep, Beep."

For a puppy, this activity might have been cute, even this late at night. However, Morgan was beyond puppy size. At the park, sure, sometimes a dog would zip around crazily for no apparent reason. I actually encouraged my pups by chasing them and making it a game, a great way for them to let off some energy. In the evening, and indoors, was not the time for this. We really had no idea what was going on, but we needed him to quit. Finally, I got his leash and tied him to the railing of the bed. At least now he couldn't barrel around the apartment. In the dark, I heard a ripping sound.

James moaned, "Now what!"

I clicked on the light and there was an orange strip of cloth hanging from Morgan's mouth. "He's eating his blanket."

James sat up and declared, "That dog is crazy!"

CHAPTER THREE

BITING THE HAND THAT FEEDS YOU

THE NEXT MORNING, I AWAKENED TO THE SOOTHING noise of Morgan snoring. Our search had ended and I was gratified. Six long months had passed since I last heard the comforting sound of a dog in the house. As soon I got out of bed Morgan jumped up and shadowed me into the kitchen, wagging his tail and ready for the day. The morning was sunny and cool so I decided to feed him breakfast out on the small patio. I thought he'd appreciate the fresh air. I loved having a dog to feed. I loved starting my day making him breakfast and observing him eat. I treasured the connection to a creature that wasn't human. Every day I had this amazing kinship that brought me such joy. I had missed it so much.

Adhering to the instructions given to us, I commanded Morgan to sit before placing the bowl down in front of the railing, then walked away and permitted him to go to his food. He greedily devoured his kibble. Too fast, I concluded, so I stepped out and pulled his bowl away, making him wait a bit. After a few moments, I put the bowl back on the ground where he gobbled his rations again.

James had trailed us into the kitchen. He believed Morgan was still eating too rapidly, so he went out onto the patio and snagged Morgan by the collar to tug him away. He leaned down and stretched out his arm to pick up the bowl. Morgan growled fiercely and bit James on the wrist. He released him and fled back inside to the safety of the apartment, slamming the sliding door and snapping the lock. Obviously shaken, he even drew the blinds.

"YOUR dog just bit me," he said angrily, holding out his wrist.

To see blood oozing from James' skin was shocking. Suddenly, the fear Morgan could hurt someone was real. Equally troublesome was the thought James would stay angry and maybe not want this dog. I'd never seen him so upset. He even canceled his morning meeting and demanded I call the rescue group.

I said I would, but waited, dreading the inevitable, certain he planned to ask them to take Morgan back. I hoped he would calm down. Disappointedly, in a stern voice he rarely used, ordered me, "Call them now."

I was relieved when the call went directly to voice mail. I left a brief message explaining the circumstances. Morgan remained outside on the patio. I felt bad for him, and for James. Was this adoption a big mistake? Did we rush because of me? In a few minutes my cell phone rang. As soon as the woman from the rescue group said hello, I immediately handed the phone to James. Not wanting to hear the discord, I leashed Morgan and we escaped the friction of the apartment. I didn't know what to do. We paced up and down the street. Was this the end of our time with Morgan? I was certain it was and I felt sad. Poor Morgan. What had happened to him? Saying goodbye to him would be difficult. Then we'd be dog-less again.

James was sitting in the kitchen reading the newspaper when we returned. His demeanor seemed calmer now. His face less angry. I asked if we were giving Morgan back.

He lowered his newspaper and said, "I didn't ask her that."

I sat down on the couch.

"She told me we shouldn't have taken his food away. That we had to be forceful with him and start to discipline him. And that if Morgan gets crazy, we have to tether him to something until he calms down."

He asked me to put Morgan back out on the patio because he needed a break. I didn't see why we had to put him out there. In this moment, I chose not to argue.

The tension remained high for the rest of the day as we spent time in separate rooms. After I sprung Morgan from his detention, I stayed in the living room writing another *Valley Voice* column about the history of Labor Day, despite how difficult it was to focus on anything except Morgan. The *Valley Voice* was a locals' column in *The Desert Sun*, the daily newspaper for Greater Palm Springs. They had already published a few of my articles.

Knowing Morgan might bite me, I was cautious as I slid down onto the floor. I gave him one of his new stuffed animals and initiated a tug-of-war. Holding onto the tail of the cat while Morgan seized the other end with his mouth, I shook the cat up and down. Morgan's head wobbled like those bobble dolls you see in cars. His ears flopped about, while his grip remained firm. The sight of his face shaking was sweet and some of my worry about him biting me dissipated, making it feel safer to shake the stuffed cat sideways, faster, and harder. Without a doubt, he enjoyed this game. Seeing him so happy made the thought of giving him up all the more depressing.

James stayed in the bedroom. The door was open and I heard him talking on his cell phone, repeating the dog bite story over and over again to a lot of different people. I heard my name mentioned several times. If only we could take back this morning I wished. After his discourse had gone on for what seemed at least an hour, I was annoyed.

Having heard enough, I walked into the room and asked James to stop rehashing the story. I was upset hearing events of the morning replayed again and again. He waved me away without pausing his conversation. I stepped back and calmly closed the door to the bedroom. No point in slamming it. This wasn't the time to escalate the stress. Besides, anger wasn't what I was feeling right then, sadness was. I was already attached to Morgan.

By the time I sat back down with Morgan, an entire leg of the cat was missing and nowhere to be found. Then I saw him chewing. "Did you eat that leg?" Uneasy about opening his mouth to pluck it out, I snatched the remaining fragment of the toy off the floor, in hopes of distracting him, so he'd drop whatever he was devouring.

At that moment, the bedroom door opened. James came out and sat in the big corner over-stuffed chair and said, "Morgan didn't bite you."

I knew what he meant. I breathed in deep and exhaled ruefully, looking at his wrist. "Does it still hurt?"

James held out his arm displaying the bite wound and said, "It'll be okay."

The cut was swollen and bruised but the bleeding had stopped. James fixated his attention on Morgan. When he saw the new toy in pieces, he seemed surprised. "Did he rip it apart already?"

"Of course. He's a Golden. That's what they do," I defended. Images flashed through my mind of all their Christmas gifts my first two dogs destroyed shortly after shredding the wrapping paper. Stuffed animals. Things that squeaked. Ultimately, I stopped buying them toys. In my opinion, sticks and pinecones worked even better for Goldens than store-bought playthings. At least they couldn't swallow the squeaker.

There was a quiet moment before James blurted out, "I've been talking to my friend Leena, and I want her to come along on our walk tonight. She rescued her dog, Wookie, and is knowledgeable about rescued dogs." Then he added, "I know you've had a lot of experience raising dogs. But I'm not convinced we should keep Morgan. He might be too much for you to handle." James wanted to get a second opinion.

Leena was the only friend of James' who had reached out to me. Whom I had begun to know a bit. She always helped with the holiday turkey. A striking Jewish lesbian from New York, who despite being in California for over thirty years, still talked fast and often. Her short, curly brown hair was rarely messed with. She knew where the best and cheapest restaurants were in all of LA. Most importantly, she adored Willy, and had been sympathetic about his passing. That being said, the undertone of James' deliberation bothered me. This was only the second day. What the hell did he expect? Morgan wasn't the only one at fault. He's the one who yanked him away by the collar. I would have bitten him, too. He didn't bite me when I took his food away. I was miffed for the rest of the afternoon.

At dusk, just before 8 p.m., we met Leena outside of her duplex a few blocks away. She told us how cute and handsome Morgan was and we exchanged hugs. Then Morgan dragged us all ahead along the sidewalk. Leena took the leash away from me and guided him back to her side. She explained the first thing you had to do was to get the attention of the dog. "Focus, Morgan. Focus," she commanded.

Surprisingly, Morgan yielded to her demand. Then we all headed down the street at a fast clip. Keeping pace with them was challenging as we approached Beverly Boulevard, full of vintage furniture stores and high-end fashion shops. We passed a new restaurant supposedly started by Barbra Streisand's son, Jason. There were always rumors about everything and everyone in LA, wherever you went.

At the next intersection, Leena ordered Morgan to sit. After she jerked the leash a couple of times, he obeyed. She pronounced,

"Making him sit at every corner could save his life. I trained Wookie to sit and now he does it on his own."

Someone telling me how to control my dog felt weird. I wondered if this meant that I wasn't a good dog owner? That maybe I hadn't really trained my first two Goldens? That I got lucky with them? And now the proof was in front of me. We waited for the light to change, then Morgan bolted ahead. She wasn't surprised by Morgan's strength and energy. She confided her dog was the same way when she first got him. I took her words as a kernel of hope.

We walked another block before she rubbed her shoulder and handed me the leash. Keeping Morgan close to me was a battle. Just as he had been on the trip to Petco, he plowed forward without noticing his surroundings. I was used to walking an older dog who insisted on sniffing everything, where coaxing him to go faster was the norm. From taking note of how Leena handled Morgan, I knew changes needed to be made with my approach.

We finally arrived at an ice cream shop called Milk, packed with young Hollywood wannabees. I know the name is about the milk in ice cream, but for me I thought of Harvey Milk. In this neighborhood hipsters wore their sunglasses at night, and it was not uncommon for a limo to show up to the curb. I sat outside at a table with Morgan, while James and Leena went in to order. Gone were the days of just wrapping the leash to a chair and knowing my dog would not cause a ruckus. Or run off. Looking around at the young crowd made me feel old. In Palm Springs, I was still considered a young chicken at the age of 51. What was I doing here?

When they came outside with their ice cream, Leena instructed us we should walk Morgan on the same route every day. You do this so the dog learns a routine. I looked over at James and cocked my head up, like a startled bird. She was surprised I wasn't doing this already, and her voice rose indicating to me I was breaking a sacred rule. Shaking my head, I sat uncomfortably and explained no one had told me this. My plan was to train him for an hour and then take him for longer and longer walks to wear him out.

"That would be the right plan for a normal puppy. You don't have a normal puppy... I think you should hire a trainer," she advocated. Leena spoke about hiring a trainer as though it were a normal thing people did every day. Like hiring a handyman. She insisted I was going to need help with Morgan and explained rescued dogs were different than regular dogs.

When I asked about the cost, she responded, "Just two hundred dollars for a couple of hours."

I leaned back in my seat; the two hundred dollars an hour charges started adding up in my mind. Two hundred. Four Hundred. Six hundred.

She looked from me to James to make her final point and declared, "I took Wookie to City Tails for private lessons and they really helped."

"That's what we're going to do." James glared at me as he spoke the words, with exaggerated wide eyes that said the decision was final.

Now they were ganging up on me. A private trainer? After twenty-five years of having dogs, I was about to hire a private trainer. This was an embarrassment. I felt humiliated. And it was "soooo" LA. Maybe Oprah. Or Ellen. Or Cher. Or anyone with one name could afford the luxury of a private trainer to come to their mansions in Beverly Hills or Malibu or Santa Barbara or wherever they lived. But not me. The whole LA scene, with designers and celebrity pet trainers and everyone wanting to be a star drove me crazy. I wished I were back home in the desert.

"Dan, I know this makes you uncomfortable," James sympathized. "Leena's right. Something happened to Morgan. Look at him. He's skin and bones. He's angry and frantic. And he bites...Your other dogs were pampered puppies when you got them. We don't know what Morgan has gone through. He needs special help right now."

I looked down at Morgan and was dismayed to see he had nearly gnawed through his new Petco leash. With deep resignation I realized they might be right.

CHAPTER FOUR

CITY TAILS

CITY TAILS WAS LOCATED ON TRENDY MELROSE Avenue, in a large two-story warehouse. Luckily, there was a small parking lot on the side, as finding a spot was never easy in this busy retail neighborhood. Upon entering the building, there was a waiting area with two benches set around a fountain and a Koi Pond. Oh boy, I thought, even dogs need fountains and Feng Shui in LA.

A woman descended the stairs from the above loft like a movie star, a diva, strutting her legs ahead of the rest of her body. Her long brunette hair parted down the middle, hung below her face. An older yellow Lab lumbered behind her. After her entrance, she introduced herself as Karena. "You must be Dan. With the problematic Golden Retriever."

"Yes, this is…" before I could introduce Morgan, he had the Lab's neck clasped in his mouth. I wrested him away and apologized. Apparently, the Zen atmosphere had no calming impact on my boy. Neither Karena nor her dog seemed upset.

Taking the leash from me she pressed for Morgan to heel and paraded him around the store, giving him treats to keep him with her. After halting, Karena stood in front of him. "Morgan, sit," she said, simultaneously raising her right hand up in front of his face, and with the other gave him a reward after he obeyed. I heard her state, "The first thing you're going to need for this dog is a training collar."

Already they had me buying their merchandise. This was going to get expensive quickly. She disappeared down an aisle and emerged with a heavy metal training choke collar. The huge spikes made me cringe visualizing them digging into a dog's neck. She took off the harness I'd bought just two days earlier and put this choke collar on Morgan. They proceeded about the store again. Morgan stayed right with her, oblivious to the change. She stood in front of him and said, "Morgan, sit." He obeyed and got his prize. She gave me the leash and a handful of the incentives and wanted me to try.

Tentatively, I took them in my hand. I had never used treats to train my dogs and I'd always opposed the use of these medieval-looking collars. But when I glanced down at Morgan, he was eagerly awaiting his next bribe. As I led him down an aisle, I resisted tugging too hard on the collar. I was not comfortable with this technique. He took advantage of the loose leash and sniffed the designer dog toys on the shelves. I rotated and stepped in front of him. "Morgan, sit." He didn't obey.

After another failed attempt, Karena abruptly announced the verdict that a group class was not going to work for Morgan right now. She told me Josh did the private lessons and he'd be back in a moment. Dismissively, she retreated behind the counter and left us standing alone. I realized we had just flunked our first obedience test and I didn't appreciate the way she deserted us. She could have and should have stayed and talked to me about Morgan. She could have made small talk. At least until whomever Josh was arrived.

As I waited for Josh, I wandered the store looking at the items they had for sale. I picked up a can of gourmet dog food from the shelf and read the label: cubes of Black Angus, grass-fed beef with a potpourri of organic vegetables and long-grain wild rice. I started to get hungry. You could have expensive squeaky toys monogrammed with your pet's initials and glow-in-the-dark leashes that played show tunes. I wasn't against these indulgences. Heaven knows, I had bought Nicholas a large Eddie Bauer, suede-covered, cedar-chipped bed back in 1983. Those days were different times. There was one store I remember in San Francisco on Maiden Lane in Union Square that catered to the Pacific Heights dog crowd who only shopped at Nieman Marcus. Unlike now there weren't groomers on every corner along with fancy boutiques selling only organic pet food. That had been my first dog and I was young and working.

Shortly thereafter, a trim and clean-shaven, thirty-something guy strutted briskly into the store. He had dark black styled hair, without any of the familiar Palm Springs-grey I'd become accustomed to. His clothes were tight fitting and possibly right off a mannequin from one of the neighborhood's trendy stores. He held his head high and seemed self-assured. He had to be Mr. Private Dog Trainer, and he did indeed introduce himself as Josh. As I explained Morgan's behavior issues, he politely nodded. When I finished, he leaned into the counter and grabbed a handful of treats from a glass jar and declared the first thing he wanted to see was how close Morgan could get to another dog before becoming aggressive. Not a good idea. I chose to keep my mouth shut and let him discover this on his own.

Josh pivoted around the counter. He motioned for the same older Lab to sit. Then he randomly dropped the treats onto the floor, in a Hansel and Gretel way, each one luring Morgan closer and closer to the innocent yellow Lab. Morgan greedily gobbled the treats before he growled and clamped her neck with his jaw. Josh heaved him away from her. I apologized again, not knowing what else to do. I felt sorry for their Lab. Josh showed no expression. He parceled out some treats and said, "Let's see what you can do."

I clutched the leash tight and let fall one treat at a time onto the floor. Wary of a fight, I didn't sprinkle any of them close to their dog. If he wanted to endanger his animal, so be it. I didn't feel comfortable doing this. Even so, after Morgan ate the last one, he pounced towards the dog where his growl escalated into a volley of vicious barks before he seized the dog's neck, again. I wrenched him off, relieved there was no blood. The ferocity of Morgan's behavior truly frightened me.

"You won the lottery," Josh announced. "An aggressive Golden. That doesn't usually happen."

You're telling me, I thought. I knew he was being sarcastic. His humor wasn't helping.

"Neither of you are ready for group classes," Josh announced. Instead, he could give me a private lesson for an hour and a half. He'd come to the house, and we'd take Morgan out and he'd show me how to handle him. "That's the first thing that has to be done," he said. "You have to take control of your dog. You can't be afraid."

Except for a fan spinning somewhere, the big, vacuous space was quiet. I didn't know quite what to say. I never expected to be in this quandary. Josh interrupted the silence by warning me, "This could be a lifestyle for the dog. Morgan may not improve. You have to decide if you want to keep him or not. Did they warn you about his aggression?"

"We saw it with one dog when I picked him up," I replied. "I didn't think his behavior would be this bad once I had him. I didn't think it would continue." I wondered what Josh was thinking about me. That I wasn't a good dog person and I shouldn't keep this animal? Or did he see dollar bills floating around me?

Gazing down at Morgan and petting his small head, I remembered when I had first seen his photo online and how I had promised that this was the one I would help. This was how I would express my thanks for everything my first two Goldens had done for me. Did I really want to go back on my word? Could I really give Morgan up? Training him was going to take a long time. But I had the time and the desire.

"Okay," I said. "When can we do this?"

Before Morgan's and my first private class, I went online to see what I could find out about this trainer guy prior to his showing up. I probably should have checked before I agreed to hire him. When I reached his website, I couldn't believe what I read. Turns out this guy was the trainer for Ellen DeGeneres and Portia Di Rossi. I shouted out, "James, you got to see this."

The news brought James rushing from the bedroom to see. He leaned over my shoulder to view the website, reading out loud the names of the stars, "Jennifer Jason Leigh! Milla Jovovich!" He grew more excited with each declaration, "Channing Tatum! Amanda Seyfried!"

He was such a celebrity chaser. All the same, I have to concede the list was impressive, including one of my favorites, Pink, who was a big gay equality supporter. James hurried to his computer to find out who Seyfried was. When he discovered she was in *Mean Girls* and *Mamma Mia,* he uttered, "I remember her."

I couldn't believe how excited he got. His excuse that movies and actors are his business wasn't convincing. James read on that Josh had been on *Access Hollywood* and the Lifetime Show *Off the Leash.* And it turns out his partner Karena, had worked with Ozzy Osborne. She was a diva. They both were.

James laughed deeply, repeating over and over again, "We've got the right guy. We've got the right guy!" He practically danced in the living room. I could feel my resistance building as he continued his chant.

"I wonder why Leena didn't tell us about his clients?" I asked.

"She probably knew that you would never go for it if she did."

She was right, of course. Before I could cancel, the doorbell rang at eleven sharp, and James leashed Morgan so he would cause less of a commotion. I buzzed Josh in and introduced him to James, who was, of course, attentive and talkative. I was bemused by his sudden interest in Morgan's training.

I wanted to say something to Josh about knowing who his celebrity clients were and asking what they were like, but I knew such questions weren't appropriate. Sophisticated LA people were supposed to act unimpressed by this stuff. By now you know being a hip Angeleno was not one of my life's goals. Once more, I digress.

He wanted to know if I'd been making any progress with Morgan. I informed him I had been practicing what Karena had showed me and was using lots of treats. I admitted I was avoiding dogs. He shook his head and explained that was just prolonging the problem. He'd show me how to deal with this when we took a walk. He wanted to know, besides the aggression, was there anything else we needed help with?

When James disclosed Morgan stole everything with his mouth and listed all the things Morgan had chewed (blankets, shoes, socks, and other people's arms), Josh obviously thought "other people's arms" was not good and the rest was just puppy playfulness. He made a point to articulate to us, "Morgan needs to learn when you say 'no,' you meant it. You decide when he plays. When he eats. When he walks. You are the masters."

Although James and I both nodded, I was uncomfortable with this attitude. I wasn't the master. Dogs were my companions. My best friends. I winced when anyone talked this way, reminding me of when people used the expression "dumb animal."

On the walk, Josh took the leash and we searched for dogs. It was a warm day as we trekked along the sidewalks of our West Hollywood neighborhood. Unfortunately, there weren't any canines around.

Usually, they were on every street corner. We walked past Urth Café, a trendy health-food restaurant, often mobbed all day long and there was only one reticent dog, tucked beneath a table, up on the patio. On any given day, there were three or four right out by the curb. I was seeing dollar bills burning into the air and I hadn't even begun to learn how to teach Morgan not to attack. At the corner we contemplated our next move. Josh considered going to the dog park, and we both agreed Morgan wasn't ready. That could be too much stimulation and wouldn't help either of us.

After another dog-less block of making Morgan sit, Josh relented and invited us to his Tuesday night obedience class. He warned there would be lots of dogs and may be too much for him. But he could at least walk me through some techniques and show me how to control Morgan.

In order to give us both time to acclimate ourselves, I arrived a half-hour early at City Tails for Morgan's obedience lessons. I wanted to be there before the place got crowded. With much relief, I found a spot in their adjacent parking lot. Having some time to spare, I walked around the store and bought an extra bag of treats. The salesclerk informed me I would have to move my truck because that was where the class was being held.

You can only imagine my string of expletives as I moved my truck as quickly as I could. Finding a spot on the street was impossible. By the time Morgan and I had rushed back, the lot was filled with the bedlam of people and dogs needing to be trained. Everything I had hoped to avoid. Despite curbing Morgan close to me, he still leapt towards the other dogs. Josh instructed everyone to line up along the wall in single file. I was able to get Morgan to sit in between my legs. There was a classmate on either side of us. I steeled myself for whatever might happen. Morgan was panting and fidgeting, looking from side to side at his canine brethren.

Josh pointed to us and directed me to go down to the end of the line with Morgan, near the rear of the lot. I was relieved to have safety at least on one side of us. Josh explained the lessons. However, at this far end, even with both hearing aids, I found it difficult to comprehend the words with the competing street noises of bus engines and trucks, motorcycles revving and cars honking their horns. You might think it odd that someone with a hearing problem would complain about noise, but since I didn't wear my hearing aids all the time, as my doctor had recommended, everything suddenly seemed too loud when I did put them in.

Josh was talking and I thought I heard the words "circle" and "walk." People turned and paraded in a small circle around two orange cones, and we joined in. Morgan eyed the other dogs behind us, so I stepped up the pace to distract him. He momentarily strode with me, then turned again.

"Morgan, sit." I stepped in front of him. When he sat, he got a treat. We repeated the action several times. Undoubtedly some of the other dogs had been there before. Several of them obeyed effortlessly. I was a little embarrassed Morgan was not better behaved. I felt I was being judged. What kind of person has a misbehaving out-of-control Golden Retriever? I understood this judgment because I might have thought the same thing. In hindsight, that I was even there with Morgan should have been a cause for celebration.

A guy with a German Shepherd must have been new, too. His dog wasn't so well behaved. Similar to Morgan, he was more interested in the other students than in obeying, and the owner didn't seem to know what he was doing, either.

I watched Josh announcing something and could hear it was time to practice sitting and staying. He said some things, but I couldn't decipher them. Once again, the other people marched in a circle. They stopped and made their dogs sit. When I positioned myself in front of Morgan to do this he lunged toward another dog.

I was losing my patience. I wasn't getting the help we needed. The help Josh told me he would give us. There was no walking me through some maneuvers and showing me how to control Morgan.

Between the street noise and the lack of attention, I wasn't pleased. Two hundred dollars for this? As we moved on to the "stay down" lesson, I tried to refocus my attention. Using a treat, I lured Morgan down to the ground. The ploy succeeded for a moment, then he popped right up. After seeing him get out of this pose several times, Josh shouted, "Keep him down even if you have to stay with him."

What he was telling me to do was to actually hold Morgan down so he couldn't get up. While this technique achieved the desired result, and Morgan stayed down, I felt scolded and singled out, and not in a good way. I would have preferred if Josh had come over to me and helped. Not shout at me from across the lot.

Class ended with mingling time, people and dogs congregated in the center of the practice area. We kept a safe distance from the other patrons. Suddenly, Morgan and a dog behind me started snarling. When I turned, the Shepherd from before approached us. I hauled Morgan away and then heard Josh shout for me to keep Morgan under control. I was startled. By both the altercation and by Josh's comment. What about the Shepherd? I wanted to say. Yell at his owner, too. My arms shaking, I was so humiliated. My breath was shallow. From my perspective, Morgan was under control. I needed to escape from that parking lot, from that trainer. Not once did he stand next to me and help. Not once did he show me how to do the exercise. After twenty-five years of having a dog, I was being forced to take obedience lessons, and I was apparently failing miserably. I wouldn't be returning to this class. I don't care how many celebrities they had. Lady Gaga herself could show up and I wouldn't return. James would not be happy.

CHAPTER FIVE

"LET'S GO SURFIN' NOW.
EVERYBODY'S LEARNIN' HOW."

ON AN EARLY SATURDAY MORNING OF THE LABOR Day Weekend we all sat outside at the Starbucks in West Hollywood sipping our lattes. The sun shone brightly, and the temperature was predicted to get warm. Two weeks had passed since Morgan joined our family. He was securely tied to my chair so he couldn't ambush any unsuspecting pooches. We were both reading parts of the *LA Times*, when James casually commented, "We should go to the beach."

"The beach?" James was referring to the dog beach up in Malibu. We'd taken Willy there a few times. I scoffed at the absurdity. He might as well have been asking me if I wanted to go to the moon. Morgan at the beach. Still, I asked, "Do you think he's ready?" We didn't even know if Morgan would like the ocean. We assumed because he's a Golden he would. I'd heard stories of water-averse Retrievers. Also, sometimes there could be huge waves at this beach that even I was afraid of. "What if there's a big undertow?" I wondered aloud, not really expecting a response. My incredulity monologue continued. "On

Labor Day weekend? . . . The beach will be mobbed. . . . Are you sure you want to do this?"

To which he responded, "Yes, why not?"

We arrived in Malibu in the late afternoon when the day had cooled off. Neither of us were sun-bunnies any longer. Getting down the cliff to Escondido Beach required descending seventy or so metal stairs, built into a square box-like staircase, no bigger than an elevator shaft. Certainly, the most unusual entrance to a beach I'd ever seen. It hugged the cliff between two buildings. Morgan was predictably hesitant. I gently coaxed him along, tugging on a long rope I used as a leash. He cautiously treaded down one step at a time. Amazing, in just fifteen days he'd gone from a fear of stairs to this display of courage.

At each landing he stuck his head through the railing and peered out into the distance. Surely, he smelled the ocean air. Hearing the crashing surf drew his interest. He turned and continued on down with more confidence and diligence. It warmed my heart to see him be so motivated. Slowly, we made our descent perfectly. He had come so far. Looking back, that Morgan accomplished this feat was a tribute to all three of us. He was trusting us more and more. He didn't even try that first day we brought him home. We must have been doing something right with him.

When we reached beach level, I praised him for a job well done. Quickly, things changed once I opened the gate to the sand. Morgan rocketed forward and suddenly I had to tightly restrain him so he wouldn't bolt away. The time for basking in our accomplishment was over. That's how things were with Morgan. One extreme to the other. One moment he was calm and the next frenzied. One moment he was lovable, the next angry and aggressive. We were learning to always be prepared for anything.

The beach was much more crowded than usual, and every group of sunbathers was accompanied by their canine best friends. Panic set in. "There's dogs all over the place," I shouted to James, who was striding ahead of me. I heard him declare it was a holiday and what did I expect?

"What did I expect?" I grumbled, loudly. "I expected the beach to be less crowded, with less animals."

He came back to me and gripped the rope and guided Morgan down to the shore. We trudged on about a hundred yards, past the landmark house-of-glass with the life-size bronzed figures and the open fire pit. As we pushed farther away from the entrance stairs there were fewer people and my disposition changed. James pointed to a spot beneath the cliff, far enough away from anyone roaming with their dog on the sand. After we set up our blanket and towels, James snatched the rope attached to Morgan and trotted towards the ocean. Morgan darted after him. When James waded out, Morgan halted at the thundering surf.

Following right behind them, I threw the tennis ball out past Morgan, aiming to entice him. He inched forward then paused as the waves splashed around him, and he scooted onshore. I urged him back out as I edged into the water, and it seemed to work. I threw the ball again while the surf was calm, hoping to lure him out. He took a few steps farther then hopped back to the safety of the sand. His ambivalence was playful and funny, although I prayed I didn't have a Golden afraid to swim. We went back and forth in this manner, until suddenly, without warning, James rushed in, scooped Morgan up in his arms, and carried him out past the rumbling breakers. Oh boy, I thought, viewing this drama unfold. Morgan looked back to me with a worried look. As though he wanted my help.

At first Morgan remained calm in his arms. However, as James plunged headstrong into deeper sea Morgan nervously began squirming. So I took a few strides out into the surf just in case, until James gently released him. At first Morgan splashed his paws frantically and his body rotated in a spinning, circular motion.

"This way, Morgan. This way!" I shouted.

After he spun around one more time, he headed towards my voice. He swam pretty well for his first try and I spurred him on as he paddled past me. His face looked anxious; nonetheless, I was pleased at how well he was doing. An upsurge crashed and he scampered onto shore where he gazed back at us, as if to say, "What the hell are you two doing to me?"

He ran back to the blanket and crouched down, where he scoured the beach for other dogs. He reminded me of a hawk perched on a branch, constantly on the lookout, peering in all directions. Judging by his reactions, he could easily spot dogs at the far end of the beach. We tried to get him to rest, even letting him lie on the blanket with us. Only there was too much to see and do. Every time we got him down, he sat up. It was right out of a Charlie Chaplin or Laurel and Hardy comedy. We spied four young poodles prancing down the beach in our direction. They were off-leash and galloped towards our blanket like the Four Horsemen. I let Morgan get close to them until he barked, then I shooed them away. They circled around our blanket. Morgan was determined to go after them. This was too much upheaval for James, who shouted for them to get away.

The owner of the dogs clearly had no intention to call them off. I should have just let Morgan go, that would have provoked a reaction from her. But four against one wasn't fair to our boy. James shouted for the woman to summon her animals. They finally retreated. You could feel them thundering away. James' voice rose an octave, which was rare, when he complained, "That woman didn't even care."

I knew it had been a long time since James had had a pet. "Welcome to the world of dog owners," I said.

Later, as the sun sank behind the cliff and a breeze picked up, I indicated to James we ought to think about heading home. He wanted to take Morgan in for a swim once more. I tagged along behind them. He seized Morgan up into his arms and waded into the cove. Out about belly-button-deep he let Morgan go and our waterdog calmly swam toward shore.

Proud parents, we both shouted, "Good boy, Morgan! Good boy!"

CHAPTER SIX

TAKE A CHANCE ON ME

BY THE THIRD WEEK, MORGAN AND I HAD ESTABLISHED a daily routine. We'd awaken early, around 7 a.m., and shuffle into the small kitchen where I'd brew myself a pot of Irish Breakfast tea and fix a bowl of organic Corn Flakes. Morgan traipsed close behind me. While the tea steeped I'd scoop out a cup of his Orijen, wild-caught, six fish kibble. I'd mix two tablespoons of organic, fat-free, plain, Greek yogurt into his and my dish.

Daytime was for Morgan. While James worked in his home office, my entire schedule was dedicated to Morgan's training. Before the temperature warmed up we'd hoof it for five blocks to the West Hollywood Park for another morning of simple "heel," "sit," and "stay" obedience lessons. I never returned to the classes at City Tails. I should have stuck to my gut feelings. I'd be two hundred dollars richer. We were now on our own and better for it.

Training a dog could not be that difficult. I raised two other well-behaved Goldens. I knew the basic commands. Years ago I attended classes every Tuesday night sponsored by the San Francisco

47

SPCA with Angel Nicholas, my first Golden. Then we practiced the lessons at the schoolyard down the street from my apartment. I'd repeat them over and over again. Afterwards we'd drive out to Golden Gate Park for some good ol' fashion tennis ball fetching. This was my goal for Morgan.

When Morgan and I had the park to ourselves, he paid close attention to me. He sat when I said, "sit." He stayed. We used two trees instead of orange cones and circled around them. He heeled well. When I reversed direction, he'd slip slightly behind me but catch up quickly and maintain at my side. I experienced a spark of hope, of confidence.

Albeit, as soon as another dog arrived, all his good behavior disappeared. Morgan could not stop fixating on the trespasser. Springing and even barking. Nothing I did could appease him. Dragging him to a different section of the park didn't alter anything. No matter how far away we shifted he continued to tug at the leash towards the intruder.

The hope I had felt turned to frustration and even despair. I truly believed his belligerency would have subsided by now. I had imagined that we would have been further along with our training. I had envisioned a steady smothering of love combined with standard training would settle him down quickly. He's a Golden for Pete's sake. Yet all my dreams proved to be naïve. We were indeed smothering him with love. Constant affection and praise were happening. Yes, his sweet disposition was appearing more often. He beamed that classic Golden smile more frequently. Occasionally, his tail aimed high. Still, if only love was the solution Morgan would already be a well-behaved companion. I was discovering firsthand that an abused animal needs time to heal.

When there was another gatecrasher, we always tried to out-wait them. Ordinarily, the human and canine would only stay about fifteen minutes, you know, to do their business, and then head back to wherever they came from. And our lessons continued. But by then Morgan was so agitated, with his tongue hanging out sideways, drooling with deep fast heavy breathing, I'd stop. On a good day, meaning without another interloper, the lessons lasted about forty-five minutes until we both became restless.

No matter what happened during this morning time at the park, afterwards we took off on a long brisk hike. We'd normally cruise on the shaded green belt that mirrored Santa Monica Boulevard, leading into Beverly Hills. The dirt path is about two miles long with plenty of places to rest and relax. Oftentimes we'd lie in the grass in Beverly Hills Park for a while and have some water and a snack. I always had to be on the lookout for another meddler showing up unexpectedly and ruining our impromptu picnic.

Obedience lessons, a long walk, and back home for lunch. That's when Morgan and I would take a nap in the air-conditioned bedroom. West Hollywood can be quite warm towards the end of summer, after Labor Day, with temperatures in the 90s. That's when the winds blew from the inland desert, bringing the hot weather. The afternoon sun shone fiercely into our not-so-well insulated apartment.

I'd let Morgan up onto the bed while I read or did some writing. I was penning a murder mystery about the Russian River based on a true crime. Hans, the German owner of the main gay bar, the Rainbow Cattle Company, had been shot to death late one night, and no suspect had ever been arrested. One reason is because the owner was such a horrible, despicable person that everyone in town hated him and was happy to see him offed. Therefore, anyone of a dozen people could have pulled the trigger.

Morgan and I would hide out in the bedroom while James concentrated in his office off the kitchen grading student papers. How warm the day was, dictated when we would venture out for our afternoon walk. Usually sometime between three and five. This outing was much more casual and without any training. Well, Morgan was in constant training to heel when I gave the command. But nothing like the rigor of the morning sessions at the park. After a rest, Morgan and I were off on another meander around our West Hollywood neighborhood. Or some variation of that schedule.

The daily marathon to wear him out may have been effective for Morgan; however, the regiment was taking a physical toll on me. By nightfall, I was exhausted, and my entire body ached. The muscles in my lower back tightened. The neuropathy flared up in the soles of my feet, and my calves burned. Sometimes my ankles just gave out and I stumbled. Nonetheless, on the days I didn't usher him out for these long endeavors, he had so much energy in the evening he flew around the house reminiscent of the first night we brought him home.

I craved the kind of relationship I had had with my previous two canine companions. The easiness of them. The protection they gave me. Acting as my good ears. Their familiarity. I was realizing that such ease and my desire for peace and quiet would have to wait. I was committed to giving a good life to Morgan, a greater cause. I would be patient. I packed my feet, or my calves, or back, with ice and rested in the evening. As I always told my doctor, the part of my body which gave me the most discomfort, received the most attention.

After a night's sleep, I always awoke resolute to build on our progress. I sincerely believed Goldens had rescued me, and I was steadfast to pay back my debt to them by giving Morgan a life he deserved. Morgan didn't know yet the travels and the adventures that lay ahead. We both had to be prepared for them.

One early September afternoon I needed a new routine, so we journeyed along Sunset, past the chic shops and the famous clubs: Skybar, House of Blues and the fancy Sunset Tower. In hindsight, I don't know what I was thinking. Cars zoomed by the loud street, busy with tour buses and honking horns. Morgan powered onward down the sidewalk with no particular focus. He didn't stop to sniff at the plants. Or the buildings. He just plowed forward. Quickly, I realized this inkling was a mistake, absolutely not the best street for either of us. But where in LA was good? I wouldn't take this route again. In fact, my adjusted strategy was to get off this street as soon as possible.

We strode further along Sunset and came to a gap in front of the famous, deco-white, Sunset Tower, where *Vanity Fair* had hosted their first Oscar night party. Adjacent was a tall, white, wrought iron gate with steps leading down to a lower area. The random staircase reminded me of some neighborhoods in San Francisco. I peered in between the bars. There was a green area down below and I saw dogs. Dogs in a dog park. I scrutinized the scene for a few moments. Should we, or shouldn't we? I didn't think he was ready. I didn't think *I* was ready. My mind accelerated as fast as the traffic. Was this an opportunity, or a colossal disaster? I studied Morgan. "You think you can handle this?" I said out loud to him. *Be brave. Be confident*, I said to myself. I wavered down a few steps. I still wasn't sure what to do. What if he injured another dog? Or he got harmed himself? What if I got bit!

I took a few more footsteps, then paused as I considered leaving, except my legs tingled from all the walking. "Forget it," a voice in my head whispered. I was exhausted from wandering. I inhaled deeply. I decided this was an opportunity I hadn't searched for. One that had come to us. Today was the day. This was meant to be. I shuffled all the way to the bottom of the staircase into the park area.

Morgan sprung towards the entrance and instantly blasted a volley of fierce barks. I tugged him in close and remained standing by the fence for a few moments to observe. He leaped forward and barked like an automatic-machine gun. "No!" I shouted without success.

There were five dogs in the park with five humans. Not too many. A manageable number, I thought, though I dreaded what might happen. I wished I weren't alone, though I wasn't sure how James would have reacted. I wanted to be a good dog owner and not charge right in with an unfriendly animal. So I cautioned everyone about Morgan and questioned if they were all right with us entering. This may seem absurd to some folks, but that's how I would want it, to give people the right impression. I didn't want to open myself up to accusations of having a dangerous dog. Of course, having a young Golden opens more gates. Had Morgan been a Pit Bull or a breed known to be fierce, I doubt the response would have been the same. The five owners voiced their support for us joining them. One woman even agreed to help. Wow, I thought, how kind and considerate. And maybe naïve. I hoped they wouldn't regret it.

Well-planned dog parks have two gates to their entrance. The first allows the animal to be safely contained inside a waiting area, so he or she can't run away before the inner door is unlatched. I opened the outside entry and Morgan darted into the holding space. With a firm leash, I unfastened the second gate and Morgan plunged through, towing me along with him. He snarled when the other dogs gathered about, and I lugged him around the perimeter of the park.

The woman who offered assistance said, "You should just let him go." I wasn't sure about this idea. I felt like a kid about to jump off the diving board for the first time. "Okay," I mumbled to myself. I opted to keep the leash attached to his collar, giving me something to grab, if I had to. I actually counted, one, two, three, then let go of the leash and Morgan bolted to the woman, slamming into her. She kept strong and greeted him. He was so excited, wiggling around her and trying to capture her arm. She smartly wouldn't let him.

Suddenly, he tore off towards another dog and knocked the animal over. I hurried behind him and jerked on the leash to draw him away. Without hesitating, Morgan sped after a second dog and tackled that one.

52

The owner snapped up Morgan's leash, shouted no and separated him from her dog. Then to me, she advised, "Just be firm with him. Goldens are smart. He'll learn." We chatted about what might have happened to him while I squeezed his leash tight. Morgan stood still, his chest thumping.

She said, "Good for you to rescue him."

The feedback felt reassuring. Feeling confident, I let Morgan go again. He hustled after a yellow Lab but she escaped to the back of the park. Morgan galloped after her. He was beautiful when he ran all out. His long ears flopped about in the forward momentum. He toppled his new love interest and they both rolled over together. With much agility she vaulted up quickly and shot back towards us. Morgan tackled her and climbed on top of her before I could pry him off.

The Lab's owner introduced herself as Cynthia. She said, "I'm okay with them wrestling. Sara likes to roughhouse. She'll let us know when she's had enough." Cynthia told me to let Morgan go. So I did. The Lab scuttled to the back of the park again with Morgan in hot pursuit. I felt such joy admiring him race so hard. His stride was long and graceful. Reversing direction, Sara flew past my startled boy. They scrambled to the front of the park and rumbled and rolled in the cedar chips on the ground. Still, I had to remain on my guard, uneasy any fuss could quickly revert to a fight. I did not want anything to happen, so I lingered as close to him as possible, just in case. Luckily, the park in West Hollywood was small and manageable. I could quickly get to Morgan wherever he was, from wherever I was.

To my surprise, I could actually see Morgan slowing down a bit. Then Sara sat to rest near the water bowls and Morgan joined her. He actually sat. On his own. I was stunned, and hopeful. Morgan was worn out, at least momentarily. His tongue drooped out the side of his mouth. His body revved like the motor of a NASCAR race car. A new sense of optimism washed over me. Maybe this kind of exercise would pan out. If we did this once, we could do it again.

Abruptly, Sara was up and skittered off once more, with Morgan not far behind. When he knocked her over and latched onto her neck with his teeth, I shouted, "Easy!" Then apologized to the owner and confessed I didn't know how to get him to stop biting that way. Cynthia waved her arm and said, "You're doing the right thing. You were on him." She shrugged her shoulders in a manner that meant - things happen. She added, "He'll just take time. He's not hurting anyone and he clearly wants to play."

When I turned on the faucet, they paused for some water. It was so gratifying to see Morgan let Sara drink before he slurped his. This was a good sign. My boy wasn't mean, and I was tickled. He was so happy to be running and playing. I couldn't help smiling at the sight of his long dangling tongue. He nudged Sara to play again but she just sat. That's when Cynthia strolled over and leashed her dog. She said, "Goodbye, Morgan. I hope we see each other again." I thanked her for her help, and she wished me luck. She was confident he was going to be a good dog.

Morgan looked a little baffled as he spotted his first friend leave. In a flash he raced after a small white dog who took refuge under a bench. That's when I realized my boy had had enough for today. No sense forcing a good thing. I was still shocked we were in a dog park at all.

At the apartment I bragged what we had accomplished. James didn't believe me at first, until he saw how tired Morgan was. He wanted to come the next time. I took my shoes off and lay on the couch. Hearing a thud, I looked up. "Did you hear that? He thudded. His first thud."

A thud is the noise you hear when a big dog's head hits the ground. The sound means, even if a squirrel ran by, I'm too exhausted

54

to chase it. Morgan had laid his head down on the floor with a thud. The same way Nicholas and Willy did, when they couldn't hold up their heads any longer. He was completely resting. My own head thudded on the pillow and I closed my eyes.

CHAPTER SEVEN

HOME TO THE DESERT

I LOVED HAVING A DOG TO CARE FOR AGAIN. TO live closely with another species helps me to connect with something greater. Reminding me every day that we are all a part of Nature. That we all share this small planet. This connection taught me that being kind to all animals is as important as being kind to my dog.

The apartment wasn't so empty now with Morgan around. I was grateful to have him to take walks with, regardless of the fact they were often precarious and wore me out. With unabated anticipation I looked forward for the day when our jaunts through the neighborhood were more peaceful and easygoing. We would find other ways for him to get exercise. We would, I just knew, and the sooner the better.

Had Morgan been a puppy we would be dealing with other issues, such as housebreaking, which would not have gone over well with James. First, his apartment was a rental. And served as his office. We couldn't have puppy urine and smells on the carpet. There's always blameless mistakes housebreaking a puppy, and James would have flipped out. Who knows how long we might have waited for a puppy?

Waiting to adopt the right dog who immediately fit into our lifestyle would have been unbearable to me. James and I often travelled between LA and Palm Springs. Occasionally, there was a trip up to San Francisco. Not to mention the yearly trip to Cape Cod. The long months without a dog had been difficult enough.

Even the simple task of preparing Morgan's food gave me immense pleasure. One morning when I set his bowl down out on the patio, he didn't wait for me to give the command that he could eat. We'd been practicing this. He seemed to be learning. When I hurried in front of him, blocking his path he bit my ankle. Immediately, I snatched the bowl off the floor and recoiled inside, shocked and a bit afraid. Not again, I thought. I sealed the sliding door and drew the blinds just to give me something to do until I could regain my bearings. Checking my ankle, I could see it was a small cut. Not as bad as James' hand when Morgan had bitten him. All the same, I was disappointed. We hadn't made progress.

After a much-needed reprieve, I realized isolating him out there wasn't fair. I undid the blinds and the door and made Morgan sit. I was mad. I felt betrayed by Morgan. How did this happen? All the effort we had put into him. The training. The walks. Waiting to eat. He knew I was unhappy. He just sat there, not moving. I had reached my limit. No matter what kind of awful things had happened to him before he came to us, enough was enough. Finally, I planted the bowl down and made him wait once again.

I was still too upset to think about how innocent he looked just resting there, acting like he hadn't done anything. Actually, that's not true. Seeing him seated there on the patio made me realize how much I loved him. I just didn't know how we were going to stop him from biting us around his food. It's not like he's hungry. He eats whenever we eat.

I finally said, "Okay, Morgan. You can go now." He rushed to his bowl and gobbled his meal. After which, he settled down.

When James came home, a short while later, I showed him the "wound" on my ankle. There was a little dried blood, but mostly a scratch. I had been so upset that I had forgotten to wash and clean the abrasion. We both agreed we had to deal with this food issue. Oddly, I wasn't afraid to wrest things out of Morgan's mouth. All the socks and toys. And yes, he took particular pleasure stealing my reading glasses. I did it all the time. But something about food made him obsessive and dangerous.

James gave me a comforting hug and helped me wash the bite with soap. He went out and brought Morgan in. My anger fully subsided when he wiggled between us. We loved him and felt bad about whatever created this compulsion. We vowed to continue to work on food. After all, he had lived with us only four weeks. Now that I was calm, I was able to reflect upon all his accomplishments. He was a champion at going up and down stairs. He quit eating his blanket. He'd been to the beach and was now an ace at swimming. Lastly, we'd had our first successful visit to a dog park.

A few mornings later, I needed to return to our home in the desert for a doctor's appointment. Morgan was coming with me. Getting an early start is best to avoid driving in the desert heat. After breakfast, I packed up the truck and wondered how our boy was going to respond to a whole house for himself, with a front and backyard, unlike living in our apartment in the city. Honestly, handling Morgan on my own, in a new location, was daunting. I wished James was coming along. He assured me he'd be there Friday, just two days away.

As I sped up the snake-like road of Laurel Canyon, through the Hollywood Hills to the 101, where I would turn south, the truck swerved and swayed. Morgan glanced over at me as though he were going to say, "Dude! Take it easy."

"Sorry. I'm going as slow as I can," I answered.

Once we were on the freeway, heading away from the city, he stretched over and pawed my arm wanting attention. Then he came near me and laid his head on my shoulder. This was the instant when I sensed that Morgan was happy to be with us. This realization warmed my soul and I felt the tension in my stomach melt away. I shouldn't have done this on an LA freeway, but no matter, I couldn't resist. I leaned into him and relaxed my head with his for a split second before informing him he had to sit up. This sweet gesture only endeared him to me even more. None of my dogs had ever done this. People had told me for Morgan's true personality to come through might take a year. His small feats were uplifting, showing how lovable he could be.

Reaching the desert by driving through the San Gorgonio Pass, which split the jagged San Jacinto Mountains to the south side, and the San Bernardino Mountains to the north was a relief. We were almost home.

The canyon was created by the San Andreas Fault. The mountains rise on either side to ten-thousand-feet forming one of the deepest crevasses in the lower forty-eight states. Those heights were the reason there was a desert. These massive granite giants blocked the winter storms and the cooling ocean air creating the dry hot conditions. Mt. San Jacinto has the fifth-largest rock wall in North America. In a wet season, snow could be seen for nine months of the year at the highest peaks.

Morgan was gazing out the window. I told him, "See that mountain up there? Someday when you're ready we'll go up there hiking and playing in the snow. Doesn't that sound like fun?" I could swear he sat up taller. Eager to go.

The awesomeness of these mountains was matched by another famous landmark of this valley, the San Gorgonio Wind Farm. As far as you could see was the future. Over a thousand windmill turbines.

Morgan had lost interest and stationed his head on the windowsill. Or maybe he was just plumb tired hearing about all the hiking and snow-balls he was going to chase up on the mountain top.

Touring through the windmills and looking up at the huge mechanical monsters was always fun. So many different shapes and sizes, spinning in different directions. Because it was the earliest commercial wind farm in operation, dating back to 1981, four generations of windmills were still operating. You could see how they'd gotten bigger, how they'd progressed from lattice design to rolled steel, and from stationary to smartly adjustable ones, turning in the direction of the wind. As the gateway into the Coachella Valley, the corridor was one of the windiest places in Southern California.

As I steered into the driveway of our residence in Palm Springs, I announced to Morgan "we're home." He acted as if he understood and hopped out of the truck and trailed me to the front door. The house was warmish and stuffy after being shut for six weeks. When you locked a house for the summer you had to leave the air conditioning set at eighty-six degrees to protect your furniture from warping in the dry heat. Eighty-six is a comparably cool temperature when the thermostat outside hits one hundred and fifteen or higher. Upon arriving, I first had to lower the thermostat to seventy-four to cool the house. Then some cold water for us both. Morgan gulped from his bowl, spilling as much as he drank. As he explored all five rooms, I wondered if he smelled Willy.

My top priority that first day back was to Morganize the house, which meant relocating anything that might end up in his mouth: the piles of papers beneath my desk, the souvenir rocks on the lower shelves of the bookcase, my one pair of expensive Palm Springs-lifestyle, Clarks sandals. I hadn't had to puppy-proof a house in over twelve years.

After lunch, we headed out to my doctor. HIV was manageable, but not forgettable. James teased me about all of my doctors and how

I regularly saw them, as if I were having multiple affairs, even if things weren't flaring up. Every organ was impacted by HIV and the meds to control the virus.

On this day I had an appointment for a rash that wouldn't go away and I needed more blood work. Since it definitely wasn't a good idea to leave Morgan alone so soon, and I couldn't leave him in the truck either, because of the heat, everyone at the office got to meet him. I know the staff loved petting him, making their day. My doctor told me to keep using the cream and the rash would clear up soon. My vital signs were all fine. "You're going to live," he joked, as we walked out of the private patient room. Although we both snickered at this common medical expression bantered by many doctors and their patients, I still had a weird reaction. Twenty-five years ago, I would have loved to have heard it. I wish someone had spoken those words to Rick when he was unwell. Now it felt dismissive, as though I shouldn't worry.

The fact is, current medications suppressed the virus and enabled us to lead healthier lives, but living with HIV isn't easy. The medicines are not a cure. If you stopped taking the pills, the virus ran rampant again. I know first-hand. I once took a medication-break for a few months to see if my T-Cells would remain high and also to give my body a chance to recover from the toxicity of the drugs. My experiment didn't work. When my T-cells plummeted, I quickly resumed the meds.

Afterwards, there was no lingering outside due to the immense heat. Undertaking a long afternoon outing was easy in LA. Not in the desert. Even if I could cope with the scorching solar rays, the pavement would burn Morgan's paws. Only before sunrise and after sunset was such an excursion advisable. In late summer, that meant after seven p.m. I waited until half past seven before Morgan experienced his first tour of the town.

Before bedtime, I set up a thick blanket for Morgan on the floor by the bed. He seemed comfortable and we both slept soundly through the night. He was still sleepy when I roused him at five a.m. We had to venture out before the sun rose. With some trepidation, I loaded him into the truck for his first Palm Springs, before-sunrise exercise. Eight months had elapsed since I was last at this dog park behind city hall on Civic Drive. I stood outside the six-foot-high, pale green, decorative wrought-iron fence and surveyed the grounds. About ten to fifteen dogs. The usual morning number.

I gazed down at Morgan and wondered if this first time might be too much for him. Or for me. I don't think he even realized where he was. This wouldn't be easy. Yet what else could I do? How could I get him enough exercise? I switched to a long leash and intended to keep a tight hold. Because of the park's huge size – over one and a half acres, the access wasn't a bottleneck. Most of the dogs didn't congregate near the opening. You could get in without the other four-legged patrons knowing.

We were keeping to the outside perimeter when a snooping beagle approached and Morgan dove for him, forcing the prowler to back off temporarily. I restrained Morgan and when the pooch revisited, I let them sniff. Morgan growled, then seized the hound in the back of the neck. I shouted "NO!" and heaved him away. The startled pup scooted off and we continued forward.

As I came upon a group of oldsters assembled in a semi-circle, I recognized some of them. I used to, on occasion, briefly be seated with them when I had Willy, who would gallivant with the other park-goers, two and four-legged ones. Now those days were long gone. I greeted everyone, and before I could even acquaint Morgan, several dogs amassed around us, causing him to roar and assault one of them. The skirmish lured others to join in. During the ensuing melee of barking and yelping, even with this commotion, the owners were unmoved from their plastic chairs. I gripped the leash and carted Morgan away.

The ruckus continued, ultimately calming down when the canine brawlers disbanded.

Charles, an older friend who I often chatted with when I was there with Willy, said, "Why don't you just let him run?"

I wasn't too keen on the notion. That had succeeded at the smaller dog park in LA where there were only five other dogs. Without a doubt, I was sure letting him go would lead to trouble here.

"Morgan's going to have to learn eventually," he added.

I know a lot of people think this way, that the dogs can figure things out for themselves. I don't adhere to this philosophy. I know my friend Charles meant well. He was always a kind and friendly guy who prized giving Willy back rubs and scratches. But he was mistaken. You don't just let them grind it out without supervision. You don't let children work it out on the playground without scrutiny to make sure no one gets harmed or made to feel bad. They didn't know Morgan's history. And just like on the playground my responsibility was to protect him and keep him safe. He'd suffered enough. I wasn't sure what to do. Apprehensively, I released the leash and Morgan sprinted to the other end of the park. Immediately, I felt this was a mistake.

"I've got to stay with him," I said, afraid someone might get walloped. I streaked after my boy who already had clamped another dog by his neck. When I reached them the Australian Blue Heeler was up and hurtled past me in the other direction with Morgan tracking him. I'd never seen Morgan run this fast, this far. I couldn't stop admiring him. How the early morning sun shone on the hues of his golden fur. How he looked so sleek and strong. Hastily, I realized this was not the time to admire him. When I caught up, Morgan and the Heeler were full-fledged fighting.

Again, I shouted "NO!" and towed Morgan off the sneering animal, allowing him to scamper away. I held the leash short and tight as Morgan panted rapidly. His tongue hung out the side of his mouth.

Drool covered his face. So I wiped him off. We proceeded to the fountain for water and a time out. He drank voraciously.

Getting a breather, I mulled over how much physical exertion this required. The situation was made worse because few, if any, of the other owners were keeping an eye on their furry friends. I wasn't expecting them to deal with Morgan but to be mindful of their own dogs. I knew full well ahead of time that this was realistically too much to expect in Palm Springs where almost everyone is retired. They surely don't come to the dog park to assume care of someone else's responsibility. They want to gather and relax and talk about themselves, or gossip about each other. Or plan for cocktails later. After about forty-five minutes I left.

Now that we were home in the desert the most important thing was to secure Morgan in the front yard. Our house was on a quiet street, without much traffic. All the same, there was no gate across the driveway. I never fretted if Willy would dash off, nor would he ever attack someone. How lucky I was nothing had ever happened to him. I was careless not fencing the yard in completely. One wrong move and a pet could get hit by a car. Or stolen. I would not take this chance with Morgan.

Since it was still morning and not brutally hot yet, I lifted several four-foot wooden stakes from behind the shed. Then I hauled out the orange plastic fence I had previously bought from Lowe's, to cordon off the front of the yard. Morgan pursued me around and inspected as I hammered the poles into the ground, starting near the street, and slid the serrated plastic through the wood. In the evening, after the sun dipped behind the mountain, I finished the job stapling the lattice to the stakes to strengthen the fence. This freed up the driveway for coming and going. No doubt, James would hate this orange fence. The first thing he'd say would be, "That looks hideous. Take it out."

Nevertheless, for that minute, Morgan's safety was secured. A more permanent solution could be discussed in the future.

Every Thursday night there is a Village Fest in downtown Palm Springs on Palm Canyon Drive. In the winter months, the snowbirds crowded the streets, dressed in Hawaiian shirts and shorts that made us locals shiver with judgment. To us, winter in the desert was cold. Only in the summer heat when the streets were empty of tourists did we natives come out in sandals and shorts and tank tops.

On this Thursday in mid-September, I decided to go to the street fair and check in with my friends at the Democratic booth. Not since June had I been around, and I wanted to find out how the different campaigns were progressing. From past presidential elections, I knew there would not be a paid position in the 2008 Obama campaign. He had California won already, so all of his money would be going to battleground states like Ohio and Virginia. So defeating Proposition 8, the initiative to ban same-sex marriage, was the campaign that interested me. The anti-8 campaign would most likely be hiring someone to organize the ground game in Coachella Valley.

Being at the Village Fest was going to be tough for Morgan. He'd go crazy. This was one of the few events where I even restricted Willy on a leash, to prevent him from getting lost in the crowd. In a cooler winter month, I could have exercised Morgan during the day by hiking up a trail or just parading around town. Then he could have been confined at home that night. But at this hot time of year, a visit to the Democratic stall would have to be part of Morgan's evening exercise.

By this election cycle I'd been working with the Democratic Party in the desert for five years. Randy, one of the dependable volunteers at the stall, greeted us, curious if this was my new Golden. While we embraced, Morgan jumped up and captured Randy's forearm. I shouted, "NO!" and opened his jaw to retrieve my friend's arm.

I apologized while he rubbed his limb and moaned, "That hurt." I emphasized Morgan was a rescue who didn't know better; he was never schooled he couldn't gnaw. While we continued to chat, a woman with a chocolate Lab wandered behind the booth. Morgan spewed like an angry voter, and I dragged him back.

Then a young girl came up and asked, "Can I pet your dog?"

"Thank you for asking but I just got Morgan and he's not trained yet." I felt bad when she shuffled away with her head crestfallen. Unmistakably, Morgan was already overwhelmed by the scene, as was I.

George, chair of the political club, inquired if I could come by the office to talk. He said they had a great game plan and he wanted me to hear about it. I agreed, upbeat to know things were happening already. As we talked some more, Morgan charged at a big white Poodle I had missed seeing and nearly trapped the animal's neck in his grip. The Village Fest would not be a layover on Morgan's Thursday night exercise route for a while. We snuck away from the crowd along a side street. I was stoked to connect with the political community again although I was uncertain if that would be possible now with Morgan in my life.

CHAPTER EIGHT

NO PAIN. NO GAIN.

JAMES RETURNED TO THE DESERT BY THE WEEKEND. On Saturday we awoke before sunrise and I shared my recent nightmare - the dog park. He laughed robustly in his infectious way, before stating, "It can't be as bad as you're saying."

Reluctantly, I confessed, "Morgan's not improving. I don't think I can keep going there. My whole body is tense when I come home. It takes a while for us both to calm down."

James suggested, "Maybe this morning will be better with both of us there."

I remained skeptical.

We road over to the field of nightmares. Besides the inattentive pet owners, another reason I was having so much distress with Morgan here was the size of the Palm Springs park. The dog park was so big, almost an entire block long, dogs could gain a huge amount of speed and momentum when chasing each other. So, when Morgan came charging from across the field excitedly thundering, the other canine park-patrons became jumpy and defensive. As soon as Morgan neared them, they fought. Also, Morgan was the new kid on the block. The other pups didn't know him. They didn't say to each other, "Who's the nut case racing around in this heat?" "Oh, that's just Morgan. Don't mind him." Hopefully, with James along, things would be different.

Once freed, Morgan barreled down to where the others congregated and misadventure promptly brewed. He picked out a big mutt to fight with. Two others joined in. The disturbance attracted more dogs who circled around, seemingly sucked into the vortex. There was growling and howling, barking and snarling. Some were squealing. Some were yelping. Plastic chairs were knocked over. Coffee mugs flew into the air. Owners scurried about to rescue their fur kids.

In the chaos, I snatched Morgan's leash and yanked him out of the melee. I trotted to the other end of the park to let the Morgan-incited disruption subside. I spotted people and dogs escaping towards the exit gate.

"People are leaving," I exclaimed to James. I couldn't prevent myself and guffawed right out loud, relieving the strain in my stomach. I detected James chortling, too. Our troublemaker kept eyeing the fleeing park-users, more than ready for another round. "Morgan really shakes things up here," I uttered. "Our little terror-dactyl."

James was still grinning as he roamed away from the entrance and the fleeing owners. Under his breath, he said to me, "Maybe this place needs to be shaken up." The frenzy was comical, yet when James inquired what we were going to do about it, I didn't have an answer.

Marion, an older woman whom I'd become sociable with at the park, came strolling our way. Willy had always given her the full "rub my belly" greeting. She had two well-behaved black Labradoodles. "Have you ever tried using an electric collar?" she asked quietly.

I wrinkled my face and backpedaled away from her and James. "I'm not comfortable with that approach."

She guaranteed me "it worked almost instantly." She pointed to her dogs. "The collar ended their skirmishing. You'll only have to use it a few times. You're welcome to try."

I shook my head vehemently. I wasn't buying into this device or narrative that discipline required pain. Marion demonstrated how it functioned. Then handed me the remote control. I pushed the start button and it shocked Marion, who was still holding the collar.

"I'm sorry," I said, sniggering, like a scene from a *Three Stooges* episode. "I didn't know if it would work." Luckily, she had a sense of humor and gave the collar to James.

As we exited, I declared, "I don't like this idea. He's been abused enough. I'm not going to abuse him. He needs love, not pain. I'm glad she got shocked."

James slung an accusation at me. "You're a troublemaker. No different than Morgan."

To which I adamantly denied, "I didn't mean it."

"I'm not convinced." He lectured, "The fighting and biting has to stop, or he will be taken away."

The possibility of Morgan being turned in for biting, and losing him, saddened me. James was right. One more occurrence might be fatal for him. He could be detained by the city's animal control and euthanized.

Returning home, James deposited the collar on the breakfast counter. We didn't employ it that night. The collar sat on the counter waiting for a day to be utilized. Not the next day, either. Nor the day after that. This terrible idea humanely lapsed.

One of the biggest pleasures of living in the desert was summer nights. We loved swimming in moonlight this time of year and "the Camp," my friend Casey's resort hotel, was the locale to go. The sun-heated pool was 85 degrees, even at the evening hour of eleven. Sometimes in July and August the water was too warm.

James wasn't sure we ought to bring Morgan there with us until I quizzed him if he knew what day it was. He pondered for a minute and when he couldn't come up with anything, I proclaimed, "The 16th. We've had Morgan for a month." We had decided August 16, the day we rescued him, would be his birthday; his Gotcha Day. To commemorate Morgan's one month anniversary with us, we agreed now was time to initiate him to Willy's home-away-from-home, "the Camp."

After a short five-minute drive, we popped into the resort from the rear entrance. The long Olympic-sized pool shimmered in blue light. Lounge chairs lined up along three sides of the pool. In the moonlight the silhouette of the ten-thousand-foot-high peak of Mount San Jacinto showed in the distance.

After I tied Morgan to one of the lounge chairs so he couldn't race around, we moseyed into the shallow end and dove. When we surfaced, not only was Morgan yapping, he had also tugged the chair over to the edge of the patio. He seemed like he was about to join us. I quickly paddled over to where he was and shouted, "That's enough!" And closed his mouth tight. "You're going to get us thrown out of here."

James swam a lap to the far end. Morgan crouched low and yelped anxiously, this time dragging the chair along to the center of the pool deck. Jumping out of the water, I latched onto his mouth again and squeezed it tightly, hoping to put an end to this new behavior.

James wrinkled his face and ordered me to keep him quiet. I repaid his impression with one of my own, and quipped: "Didn't it look like I was trying to? What do you think I was doing? Brushing his teeth?" Basically, our efforts weren't succeeding. Morgan just became too excited when one of us did a lap. Maybe he felt neglected. None of my other dogs had ever misbehaved in this manner, anywhere. We had expected "the Camp" to be a good playground for him. The large open-aired complex was completely enclosed. We never knew what was going to happen with Morgan, our problem-child. We loved him in spite of the fact he caused a lot of clamor and presented unique challenges we weren't always prepared to deal with. James climbed out of the water, and we assumed turns staying with Morgan while the other swam a lap. We were lucky there were no other guests during the week.

Just then a tennis ball sailed through the air and landed at the far end of the pool. Morgan plunged into the water before I could catch his leash. Angrily, I glared back at where the ball came from, wondering who would do such a stupid thing. Pets weren't allowed in public pools, and we had been struggling to make sure Morgan obeyed the rules and didn't go in. When I glimpsed Casey, the owner, standing there, beaming ear to ear, I knew things were fine. Casey had always encouraged me to let Willy take a dip when there were no guests around, and I never took him up on his offer. I was always afraid that it would teach him that he could go in the water whenever he desired to. I didn't want to encourage him. Now there was Morgan swimming to the end of the giant pool where the ball was and retrieved it, heading to the side wall. "This way Morgan," I hollered. He didn't seem to understand. James swam over to our splashing boy and positioned him correctly towards the stairs.

"I saw you come in on the video monitor and heard Morgan barking," Casey said.

I told him about our one-month celebration with Morgan, who then rushed over near Casey and shook off the water. Casey laughed and confiscated the ball out of Morgan's mouth and lobbed it back into the far end of the pool. This time I could enjoy admiring Morgan paddle to the end. Again, he swam to the side to get out; this time, James was ready for him and aimed him towards the steps.

As I look back and consider the ordeals we faced with Morgan, I realize how fast we did things with him. What would Morgan's life have been like with different owners? With people who didn't take him to the beach to swim? Who didn't bring him to the park to run? With people who just limited him to the backyard or only on a leash? Reflecting now, I know we rushed him. We wanted him to fit into our lives. *We wanted him to be like Willy.* We didn't want to delay until he was ready. When would that time come? We wanted his life to be full and exciting. The LA trainer claimed in order to break his aggression he had to be around dogs. Well, wouldn't the same apply to being at the beach? Or the park? In order to know how to behave at those venues he had to be there.

CHAPTER NINE

TO THE COFFEE SHOP WE GO

WE OPTED TO FOREGO THE DOG PARK FOR A FEW days and instead introduced Morgan to Koffi, the coffee shop where James and I first met. We knew we would have to keep a careful eye on our boy. The large grassy quad had several entrances so clientele had different walkways into the complex. Koffi was known as a very dog friendly business. Some people treated the grassy knoll like a dog park. An off-leash one. I have to disclose, I used to be one of those people. Willy had free-range of the area. In my defense, this was just after the cafe opened, before the place became a hot destination. Now every other customer brought a dog.

We also needed to limit the number of people who might try to pet him. So often someone would spy Morgan from across the way and traipse right over to us. Even some with children in tow. I call it the Golden Curse. People spot a Golden and think it's open season to lay their hands all over them. Even with Angel Willy this bothered me. I understood and accepted it to a point. Having a Golden is a special thing. Not everyone gets to be owned by one.

We situated a table in the rear, far from the front entrances. Experience taught us that most people stayed within a few yards of the front door. James went to purchase our drinks. I'd just settled Morgan on the lawn when sure enough a woman eyed him and immediately tramped our way. I extended my hand out and asserted, "Please no. He bites."

"Oh, he does not. Goldens don't bite."

"This one does," I countered, slightly irritated that she challenged me. Little did she know. "He's a rescue. We just got him. We're trying to keep him calm."

I could see she wasn't yet persuaded.

I felt guilty. The truth is I just didn't want to be disturbed right then and there. "Please don't," I said firmly.

With a huff, she turned and stomped away. Why do I always feel so guilty when I say no and establish my boundaries?

Not more than ten minutes later I had a do over. Another stylish lady came into the courtyard and noticed Morgan. She headed in our direction, but then halted halfway. "May I come and say hello to your pretty boy?"

"He's a rescue. Sometimes he bites," I revealed to her. "But thank you for asking."

"Of course. I had a rescued Golden like that," she informed me.

James showed up with our iced teas. "You did?" he exclaimed. Suddenly we were now captivated in what she had to say.

"Yes. He was really crazy when I first got him."

"We can't let him near any dogs. He's so aggressive," I reported.

"I understand. It takes time for things to change."

"At night he races around the house. Like a crazy dog," James chimed in.

She smiled. "Mine did that as well. When I first got him. I'm Monica. By the way."

"He did?" James pointed to himself first and then me. "James and Dan. And this is Morgan…Did he ever stop?" James inquired.

"He did. Eventually. Does he have a place that's just his?"

"The whole house," I broadcast with a chuckle.

She laughed at that. "I mean a special place that is just for him to rest in."

"You mean like a crate?" I queried.

"Or a portable kennel. Some place where he can lay down in and watch everything. That made a huge difference for my rescued boy, Jake."

"He doesn't," I acknowledged. "I've been reluctant to get one."

"Maybe we ought to think about it," James said. "Would you like to meet Morgan?"

"I'd love to. Thank you," Monica stated. She slowly paced across the lawn and knelt before him. "Hello, Morgan. Nice to meet you." She regarded James and me and articulated, "You really have a special Golden. May I pet him? He's gorgeous. He must have come from good stock."

Morgan lifted his head.

"Of course. You think so?" I probed.

"Oh yes." Monica gently guided her hand over the top of Morgan's head and down along his shoulders. "His coat is beautiful. All those different blond colors. He's really special."

"We have been so concerned with training him and calming him down, we're not sure about those things," James cited.

"You can be sure." Monica stood. "Try a crate or a kennel. See if that helps him. It made a huge difference to Jake."

"Thank you. Thank you so much," I said.

Monica wished us good luck as she ambled away. Our conversation lifted our spirits. We welcomed any positive news we could get. I feared that buying a crate would be for a one-time use and then be discarded, such as the harness and the medieval choke collar.

We sauntered our way back home before the day became too warm. We weren't swayed a crate would be worth the money. Just as we entered the house, I had an epiphany. "I have Willy's portable kennel in the shed. All I have to do is clean it out. Everything's all there. The bolts. The door. Everything."

James was thrilled to hear this news. Going to the shed was always bittersweet for me. Willy's grave lay just a few feet off the path on the right. I always paused for a moment to say, "Hello Willy. I miss you, baby. Always." Today I added, "I'm getting your kennel out. We're going to use it." I'd reminisce about something fun we did together like a refreshing swim in the Russian River on a warm afternoon. Where I'd toss a ball out to the center and we'd both swim after it.

I dug out the kennel from the back of the shed. After a thorough cleaning and drying, I placed a blanket inside and we were ready for a test drive. But before we began, we agreed to remove the door. Morgan wasn't going to be caged. The space was to be all his own, where he could come and go as he pleased. At first Morgan held back, far away from the crate, even with coaxing. However, the moment I tossed a ball in, he scampered after it and quickly turned around and came right back out. I considered the trial run a success. "What a good boy, Morgan!"

We did this for a few tries and in time Morgan was slower to scuttle back out. In the evening, James and I enjoyed watching the local evening news. Morgan had other notions. He wanted attention. Even despite taking him for exercise twice a day, early morning and again after the sun went down, he still had so much energy. So, we invented a game called, "Morgan get in your cage!" We'd chase him around a little bit and then shout, "Morgan get in your cage!"

He'd bolt inside and zip back out. It made me smile so much and I sensed myself loving him more and more. Training him was sure a lot of effort, twice as difficult as Willy. Who am I kidding? Ten times more difficult than Willy. I could see James was feeling the same way. Willy was always my dog and my responsibility. Morgan is the first dog the two of us raised together, as a couple, as co-parents. With Willy, James was the stepdad. The interloper. The competition for my affections. I rarely saw James play with Willy. That wasn't the circumstance with Morgan. James crouched on the floor and played the game whole-heartedly. It was touching to watch the two of them. Let me tell you, taking care of Morgan required both of us. He was way too much for one person. I don't know how one person could have raised him. I can't imagine Morgan having a good fun life without two people handling him.

Unquestionably, when Willy became stricken with Lyme's disease on Cape Cod, James was the one who took the lead in getting him treatment. While I was still in denial and overwhelmed that my beloved boy was seriously not well, and maybe dying, James made the decision to treat him.

To see James crawling on the floor, play-demanding Morgan to get in his cage, made me smile. Then I sat next to the kennel and when Morgan raced in, I gently blocked his exit and made him sit down. I petted his head and doled out a treat. He calmed down a little. Then we decided to use one of his own favorite pastimes – we put an old newspaper in the kennel. Straightaway he sprang to the task of shredding the pile. He took a while to complete his mission and afterwards he definitely was a little worn out. Monica's advice seemed to be an effective remedy. This gave us a few minutes to indulge in our program peacefully, without him seeking to get our attention.

James and I alternated turns reloading Morgan's pile of tearing supplies. We had plenty of old newspapers on hand. In the ensuing evenings, Morgan was slightly less wild. He necessitated fewer newspapers to shred before he was tuckered out. We particularly relished the times when he sat half in the kennel and half out, which was a happy compromise as far as we were concerned. We learned to extol all the little victories with Morgan. And eventually got to watch the evening news from start to finish uninterrupted by you know who.

CHAPTER TEN

THE CAMPAIGN OFFICE

THE DEMOCRATIC CAMPAIGN HEADQUARTERS WAS AT a modest street-level office at the south end of Palm Canyon Drive. Behind the building ample parking was available for volunteers. George, Chair of the Stonewall Democratic Party, gave me a tour around the office. The usual front area where the public entered had a desk, a coffee maker, a fridge, and a copy machine. In another room was a ten-foot-long table where the volunteers would be trained.

In the rear of the office was an alcove with a large district-wide map hung on the wall with pushpins in specific locations, indicating neighborhood precincts with activity already happening. Another large closet served as storage for signs, reams of paper, and stacks of literature and brochures. After working on dozens of campaigns from presidential to city councils, I was very familiar with the set-up.

I had expected to be hired on "No on 8," the campaign to defeat a state-wide ban on same-sex marriage. George explained, "No on 8" wasn't organized thus far in the desert." Instead, I would be assigned to the U.S. House Congressional candidate, Julie Bornstein, a Democrat, who I liked. She was running to unseat Mary Bono, Sonny Bono's widow. Originally a musician, Sonny was best known as the partner, with his then-wife, Cher. The two starred in the Sonny and Cher Show, a television hit in the 60s and 70s. After the show was cancelled and the couple divorced, Sonny relocated to the Coachella Valley and became involved in local politics. He served as the Mayor of Palm Springs from 1988 through 1992 and was credited with restoring the town back from neglect and obscurity, creating, among other booster projects, the Palm Springs International Film Festival. Bono was elected to Congress as a conservative Republican in 1994. When he died on January 5, 1998, in a skiing accident at Lake Tahoe, his second wife was elected to complete her husband's term. She had served since then and had married a colleague, a congressman who represented a district in Florida. Now known as Congresswoman Mary Bono-Mack, she referred to herself as a moderate but had voted along Republican Party lines ninety percent of the time.

George assured me that although we would be executing for the Congressional race, "we'll also contact voters about Obama and Prop 8." He elaborated further, "The Prop 8 campaign would eventually open their own operation." He clasped his hands together in a matter-of-fact manner. "In the meantime, we would be the only game in town."

Though Morgan was home at the time, I pronounced, "My one request is that I bring Morgan."

George smiled and remarked, with a wave of his hand, "Of course. I suspected that would be one of your conditions. Didn't Willy always come to the office?"

On my first morning at the campaign headquarters with Morgan, without a moment's hesitation he popped up and grasped everyone's arm with his mouth, like a puppy. No one felt threatened, but he couldn't persist doing that in this professional environment with volunteers coming and going. By luck, my desk was secluded in a side cubicle. When I had to leave to use the photocopy machine, located in the front reception, I fastened Morgan to my chair. Since all copy machines are a bit distinctive and temperamental, I took some time to learn how this one operated. When I heard a bark from the other room, I shot in with a firm, "No!"

I proceeded back to the machine to read the instructions. To my surprise, Morgan materialized in the doorway of the reception with the chair still attached to his leash. His tail wagged and his black lips were curled up to form a joker-type smile. He was proud of his accomplishment of making it this far. I had to temper my chuckle. He could not be encouraged. "Morgan, you can't do that here," I counseled him softly, then carted the chair and him back to my space. "Now stay." I reverted to my copying task and within seconds Morgan reappeared, along with the chair. This time I wasn't amused. "Okay, this isn't going to work."

George calmly recommended, "Maybe Morgan needs to be tied to the desk for a while?"

I agreed. It's also why I agreed to work with George. He was calm and always looked for solutions. Once again, it required some adjustments to see what Morgan's limits were and how I could still do what I needed to do. The fact is, I wasn't there to spend time disciplining my dog.

The next morning, Morgan was less troublesome. I labored at my desk updating the volunteer list on my laptop. This campaign was the first I'd ever used one. I felt so hip and modern, though I'd heard a lot of Obama volunteers across the country had discarded their laptops and were using their cell phones to record voter information. As I toiled, Morgan lay by my chair. Now and then I generated a few phone calls about the database system. Unfortunately, I was easily distracted while listening carefully to the volunteers. Hanging up, I glanced down to find Morgan gone. The only remnant was a small section of a chewed leash.

I hurried into the front to find him sitting by Joni, a familiar volunteer from past elections. "We were just talking," Joni stated, as she petted his head. "He's as sweet as Willy."

Her observation was gratifying to hear but I didn't feel that way just then. I replied, "Morgan's a monster. Don't let him grab your arm."

She waved me away and added, "He tried that already. I wouldn't let him."

At the end of the day, I drove to Petco and bought a chain leash. I hated how heavy and noisy the links were, nevertheless, he couldn't chew through metal. Or at least I hoped he couldn't.

Evidently, I had to find a better way to keep Morgan entertained at my job. I couldn't keep giving him rawhide chews. Too many weren't healthy. Experience taught me one thing he delighted in doing was ripping apart paper. Any kind. So I supplied a steady stream of old newspapers flowing beneath my desk. Morgan lay down and I heard him shredding. In the evening, the floor surrounding my workstation looked like a blown-apart trash area but at least Morgan had been quiet, and I'd done my job. As long as I cleaned up the worse of the mess, I figured no one was going to object.

For about a week, letting him destroy newspapers proved to be the best way to keep him calm. Anyhow, when I arrived at the office the next Monday morning, I was given more responsibilities. My job now included instructing the volunteers. Since the coaching was done in the rear conference room, I wasn't going to be able to babysit Morgan. This meant I would have to leave Morgan alone at my desk, or someone would have to keep an eye on him. As Election Day inched closer, more and more volunteers would drop in, and I would be even busier. I made an agonizing decision. I had to leave Morgan home.

I hated being away from him. I was dissatisfied and upset that this was the solution. I'd never had to leave my other dogs alone before while working on a campaign. Regardless, Morgan just wasn't capable of being a campaign mascot. Part of me felt like quitting, even if the extra money helped, but the election was so crucial. I was motivated to pitch in on this historic campaign. I loved getting the No-on-8 signs out around town. Our impact was happening, our signs were displayed in front yards. On business windows. On street corners. I even got the Desert AIDS Project, an organization that steers clear of political campaigns, to display a sign outside their campus. I intended for the local bigots to know this was our town now and they had better keep their hatred hidden.

Separating from Morgan on the first morning was excruciating. I really felt like I was abandoning him. I empathized with the way a mother might feel when she left her child behind in the morning for a job. Each day I rode home at lunch to let Morgan out for a bit and to interact with him, so he wasn't deserted the entire day. On one occasion I had to answer a pressing call of nature. When I returned from the bathroom, I couldn't find him. I noticed in my urgency I had neglected to close the front door. And even worse, I had left the orange barrier down also. Morgan had fled out of the yard and down the street. I glimpsed that the elderly man with the "Rush is Right" bumper sticker on his old pickup truck held him by the collar.

"Is this your dog?" he asked, gruffly.

I took hold of Morgan and said, "I left the door open and he got out."

It stunned me when he grumbled, "Your dog bit my arm."

I saw the blood and remorsefully apologized, "I'm so sorry. Can I take you to the hospital?"

He flailed his hand away and claimed, "I'm all right."

When your dog has had another person's arm in his mouth you apologize profusely and disappear as fast as possible. My body trembled from the incident. The stakes are so high. This man's injury was my fault. There was so little room for error with Morgan. I had to be more aware. One mistake and he could be in deep danger. He could be reported, dispatched and euthanized. This would be devastating. I couldn't bear the notion of that loss.

It was hard to remain mad or disappointed with him. After I brought him inside, I squatted on the floor next to him. He appeared oblivious to the episode. He was probably elated he had escaped for a while. He may have reckoned his breakout had been a game. In so many ways, I was out of my comfort zone. Occupied on this campaign was a big delay in Morgan's training and I felt guilty. I vowed as soon as the election was over, I would find Morgan a class for him. I wrapped my arms around him. "Just a few more weeks, Morgan," I whispered. We could both hang on.

One night after work, when leaving the house to take Morgan for his exercise, I bumped into Lonny and Bill, the couple from next door. I explained the late hike and they were shocked to learn I wasn't bringing him to the office. Hearing this, Lonny volunteered to mind him. Her generosity caught me off guard and at first, I agreed. The more I weighed their offer, the more uncomfortable I became with this arrangement. My gut feeling told me this was a mistake.

Something about these neighbors disturbed me. Lonny had an extremely high-pitched voice. I'd never heard anything like it before. Something wasn't right. And her husband? All he babbled about was how much crime there was in Palm Springs, which was completely unfounded. By this time I'd lived in Palm Springs for five years and nothing had ever happened to us and as far as I knew to them either. His paranoia was definitely a red flag for me. As hard as I tried, I couldn't think of a way to get out of their offer without insulting them.

Ultimately, I supposed entrusting Morgan with them was worth a try. I mean, what could happen?

The next morning, I delivered Morgan to them and to my distress, that night when I retrieved my boy, they informed me he had growled at Lonny and bit her. I didn't want to believe them, until she revealed her leg and I observed the red and blue teeth marks. Thankfully, he didn't break the skin. My heart sank. That option abruptly ended. I apologized repeatedly. I even went out and bought her a bouquet of flowers. No matter what I tried, I hit a wall. I didn't know what to do. Again, her bruise was actually my misjudgment since I never should have permitted Morgan to stay with them. I should have trusted my gut about leaving him with these neighbors. I should have heeded my intuition even if that offended them. Morgan was my priority, and he simply was not ready to be babysat by anyone.

When James and I first met, on a few occasions, I left Willy overnight with my friends, John and George. They had other dogs and also a pool. Okay I admit. I was a little stung when he hopped out of the truck and zipped for their door without even turning to peek back at me. But why not? Willy's eagerness made me smirk. What Golden wouldn't want to go to doggie day care where there's a pool and friends? It became apparent this might never happen for Morgan. Could I ever let him have a sleepover? Could I even let someone else walk him?

My life was changing with Morgan. I had made a deep commitment to him which meant I was responsible. Maybe adopting him was a mistake? Maybe he was too much for me? Did I really want to forego the things I was passionate about, like my activism, that brought me a sense of accomplishment?

I had to make a decision as tough as it may be.

CHAPTER ELEVEN

A PLACE JUST FOR MORGAN

SATURDAYS ARE ONE OF THE BUSIEST DAYS IN a political campaign, starting early and bustling non-stop until late afternoon. On this particular Saturday in October, the alarm clock read 7 a.m., and my body pleaded to nestle in bed with the covers over my head. The bottoms of my feet were inflamed. My lower back was tender. The tightness in my lower stomach ached, and I wasn't sure whether a bladder infection was flaring up or just the usual nervousness of an election. All this discomfort caused a headache which throbbed intensely when I inserted my hearing aids in my ears.

With previous campaigns, I usually could endure several weeks before feeling this run down. I questioned whether my fatigue was from getting older, or a symptom of my HIV. In fact, the way I felt that morning forced me to concede to the possibility this will be my final campaign, and melancholy washed over me. At that moment Morgan padded over to my side of the bed and lay his head upon the mattress, maybe sensing something was wrong. I rubbed his head to reassure him I was okay.

I took pride in my work for its contribution to our American democracy. Politics was in my blood. As a nine-year-old boy, I was thrilled when my grandmother's brother, Mike Flaherty Sr., ran for a seat in the Massachusetts House of Representatives from South Boston, back in 1966. In my mind I can still recall the day we put a large "Elect Mike Flaherty" sign beneath our second story apartment window that could be seen from blocks around the park. Throughout the campaign we stood outside Tuckerman Elementary School, urging parents to vote for him. I still cherish how proud everyone felt when he won.

James and I talked at length about our Morgan dilemma. He didn't support me resigning from the campaign to tend to our boy. He offered to shift his office out to Palm Springs for the final weeks before Election Day, to lighten my stress and babysit Morgan. This made all the difference, and not just for Morgan. I was particularly grateful when James dropped by the office with lunch and a happy dog.

One morning, when I was sluggish to rise, James brought Morgan to the dog park early; within the hour, he emerged in a fury. He slammed the keys down on his dresser and roared, "I am never going there again."

As you know by now, James rarely got visibly upset, so I leaned up to hear what had happened.

"Another dog attacked Morgan and the owner did nothing." James removed his pink linen shirt and continued. "I shouted at the woman and she just sat there, even after her dog bit me. I hate that place." He bared the mark on his arm and declared. "Everything you said about it was true."

I climbed out of bed to comfort him. I wrapped my arm around his shoulder.

"We are never going back there," he proclaimed, a second time.

And we never did.

A few days later I was surprised when James waltzed into the office with Morgan along with my favorite black tea latte from Koffi and a chocolate croissant.

"That's mighty considerate of you," I expressed. "Thank you."

Then he heralded, "I'm taking Morgan for a hike with Peter and Ivy."

I rose from my desk. "You're taking Morgan with another dog?" I knew Peter's dog. She was big. Huge, in fact. A Rhodesian Ridgeback. I recognized that the tea and croissant were a bribe.

According to James, Peter assured him it would be fine. Peter was the man with whom James had produced a film about Victor Kravchenko, who exposed Stalin's forced collectivization of Ukraine in the 1930s, killing millions of people. We always nicknamed Peter "the Ukrainian."

I shook my head. "I don't like this idea. Ivy's going to injure Morgan in a fight." Dissuading James was futile. I had lost this debate before it even began. James was going. "Please don't let him off the leash. He'll run away." When he agreed too quickly, I knew I'd lost that debate, too. I pursued them out to the car. I implored James, "Please don't. How are you going to feel if Morgan runs away?"

James continued to agree with me and I realized he had made up his mind. I obsessed about them for the next few hours.

Later in the evening, James shared that Morgan's new girlfriend, Ivy, wouldn't tolerate any crap from him. When he acted up, she just socked him with her paw and he quit. James swiped the air with his hand imitating Ivy. I could tell he was excited about this new secluded canyon to bring Morgan. He rarely used his hands in that Italian sort-of-way when he spoke, and often made fun of me when I did. Apparently, the two dogs had run and run. Proof of this exertion was how quiet and calm Morgan was that night.

"I wish I'd have been there to witness this."

"We'll go tomorrow. I'm sure we've found a place just for Morgan."

"And you let him off leash." A statement, not a question.

"Peter said it would be fine. [Fine? I rolled my eyes.] Ivy had minded Morgan and kept tight tabs on him." James expounded, "Morgan would follow her, and when Peter called Ivy, she came directly with Morgan in tow." (I doubted this.)

I sprawled down by our boy and stroked his big head. "Did you have fun with Ivy? Did that big girl knock you around?" Morgan lay there, panting, with his tongue hanging low.

The next morning, James and I were up on the trail by 8. There was a dirt footpath which curved around boulders of all shapes and sizes and brush-like smoke trees, chollas, and brittlebush, heading into the Las Palmas Canyon. I maintained Morgan on a leash through the entrance area. The valley was shaped in a half-moon. The first thing you discovered was a twenty-five-foot-high wall of giant boulders acting as a dam to divert storm runoff water protecting the expensive homes in the lower neighborhoods. This dam extended the entire length of the valley forming an enclosure.

James signaled, "This is where we can unleash Morgan."

I wasn't so sure. I was bothered to no end that Morgan might sprint off. I surveyed the vast open field before us and speculated what may possibly be out there that we couldn't distinguish. Rabbits and birds, for sure. Hungry coyotes used the trails in their hunt for food. Bees had been known to attack hikers. In the summer, black-and-white California king snakes, red diamondback and speckled rattlesnakes slithered across the trail to warm themselves. Then there were the most dangerous species: other humans with their dogs.

With James' encouragement, I released Morgan. He bolted off onto the trail. I spied him darting between the barrel cactus, smoke trees and rocks with his head bent low sniffing the ground. It was the first time I'd seen him track like this. On occasion he'd turn back and stare at us. Standing tall, his body firm and muscular. His ears pushed back. His bushy tail curved up. Then he tore into the brush and momentarily disappeared when I saw quail and doves scattering about and flying off in all directions, I knew where he was.

We were at the base of the rocky San Jacinto Mountains towering above the desert. The cathedral wall of the mountain, peaking ten-thousand-feet into the sky, made me feel small. I found it easy to get distracted among this raw, awesome beauty of the desert landscape. But I understood I had to keep my eye on Morgan.

We reached the far end of the half-moon valley. I hollered out his name and he came scampering out of the brush to our side. Astounded that he returned, I said to him, "What a good boy you are!"

"You must feel relieved?"

"I am. I like this place. And clearly Morgan does, too."

James pointed to a ridge higher in the canyon and described, "There's a wide, flat, table-boulder up there where we can sit."

"Let's do it."

We trekked up the slope. Morgan sped ahead of us like he instinctively knew where he was going and was eager to get there. Then hurried back to us as though he were wondering what was taking us so long. "Are you having fun?" I queried him. His enthusiasm made me smile. I struggled a bit with the climb since I was out of shape and my body wasn't rested.

We perched on the boulder overlooking the desert floor and marveled at the sight beyond. There was a haze hovering on the horizon. Green fan palm trees dominated the view below. The windmills slowly rotated in the north. In the distance, the white desert sand stretched for miles, until blocked by the Little San Bernardino Mountains, enclosing the Coachella Valley. Morgan gazed at the vista and lounged between us on the cool, flat, grey granite rock. Once again, we felt like a family completed. We had found Morgan and now we had found a place just for him.

CHAPTER TWELVE

GRATEFUL FOR THE LITTLE THINGS

IT WAS PRETTY CLEAR WE WOULDN'T DEFEAT Congresswoman Mary Bono-Mack. She refused to debate Julie and had over a million dollars to spend to our four hundred thousand, not nearly enough to unseat an incumbent. To Bono-Mack's credit she was good on animal issues. Hope lingered for both Obama and Prop 8. On election night, when Obama was projected President-elect and came out on stage to speak to the crowd of supporters in Chicago, tears filled my eyes. To witness and be part of a historic moment was awesome. The American story had been rewritten. I was so proud of our country and everything it stands for. We were truly on the path for a more righteous union. As the election results of the ban on same-sex marriage filtered in, my euphoria was dampened with dejection and anger.

Generally, after every campaign I participated in, I crashed after Election Day, even if we won. Losing Prop 8 hurled me into a despair I hadn't undergone since the 2000 Gore campaign, with the Florida recount and the Supreme Court ruling giving the presidency to Bush. This loss was different. This was more personal. This was a direct assault on my own civil rights. I was sorely disenchanted with the people of California. We as a community had lost this campaign in so many ways, and I was prepared to tell anyone who would listen. The best thing for me to do was to get out of town, so James, Morgan and I spent a week at his apartment in West Hollywood just hiding out and needing time off.

While in LA, however, we chose to join the planned protest against Prop 8. How could our civil rights be voted away? How could anyone's? We decided to bring Morgan along. This would be his first demonstration. We weren't sure how he would do with all these people shouting and chanting. While unlikely that any violence or hostility would occur, nonetheless, we vowed that if things got out of hand, we would slip away quickly. We were pleasantly surprised when a line of protestors formed to pet Morgan and take their picture with him.

Gradually, after a few days, my anger veered to sadness as I assessed if my time campaigning was over. Despite the stimulating excitement while laboring on campaigns, the work exhausted me. I also realized with ample amount of rest, my spirits would rebound. And they did. One morning I awakened and regarded Morgan asleep on my side of the bed. Observing him made me smile. My new campaign was hairy and had four legs and lots of energy. Committing to Morgan excited me. I was zealous to bestow upon him my undivided attention.

As Thanksgiving was upon us, our focus turned toward home. We were uneasy about the holiday. We were apprehensive how Morgan would react to all the people in his house. Then, James' friend, Leena, requested if she could bring her rescued dog, Wookie, a suitably named frizzy grey mutt, a little smaller than Morgan. At first, I cringed, I did not want this to happen. Hosting a large group was demanding enough for me, having another nut case skirmishing around was more than I could manage.

After a few days, I had a change of heart. I commiserated with her when I found out her longtime relationship had ended; she only had joint custody of their dog Wookie every other weekend and she missed him terribly. I was still perturbed by her glowing endorsement of City Tales and the personal LA dog trainer, yet she really was the one person who had helped us with Morgan. I appreciated her empathetic concern and believed this would be a way to thank her. Not to mention, she was handy in the kitchen. So even if I wasn't sure he was ready, she was overjoyed when James informed her, "Wookie is welcome."

Was I being fair to Morgan? He was our responsibility. One I took seriously. We had to put him above all else. We all agreed if the boys got out of hand, Leena would put Wookie in her car for a while until things calmed. I was not going to confine Morgan to the bedroom in his own home. That would not happen. Leena understood this.

The arrangement was for the two misfit boys to meet outside, in the front of the house. After a couple of scuffles where Leena and James played referee, they seemed to resolve their differences. The real test came when we put them in the backyard where they enjoyed free-range including the back sun porch. They sped inside and sat next to each other in front of the retractable gate prohibiting them from entering the house.

Then Leena spoke, "Look at them! I can't believe how much Morgan has changed."

"I'm not sure I know what you mean," I replied.

"He's so much calmer. And not so crazed. He's paying attention and listening. I'm really surprised how different he is. You did all this in just four months. Congratulations for doing a great job."

I was delighted to hear this, "Well thanks. It's difficult to see. He's still so much work."

"I understand that. To see the change in Wookie was hard for me too. But look," she pointed at the two of them on the back porch. "That never would have happened when you first got him."

"It's a miracle!" James proclaimed.

I rolled my eyes. To him miracles were everyday occurrences. Everything was a miracle. Getting a film made was a miracle. Swerving out of the way of a car was a miracle. Oftentimes I laughed at him. If a song we both fancied played on the radio, I'd gleefully blurt out, "It's a miracle."

"You're mocking me," James objected.

And I'd giggle. If the truth be known, I secretly admired his optimism and positivity. I may not see miracles everywhere but who was I to put his belief system down? My life has been atypical. I can't help asking, where was the miracle when Rick died in 1987? Where was the miracle when so many of my friends were sick and dying back in the 80s and 90s? If good things were miracles, what were the devastating things called? The remnants of that horrendous era endure with me. Nonetheless, I dreaded to consider what our relationship would be like, if we were both glass half-empty people. Not a good one. One of us had to be positive. His optimism tempered me, prodding our relationship forward.

Leena's validation was comforting. You might think this was a strange word to use for this situation, but Morgan's improving demeanor impacted me in so many ways. First, there was now hope that Morgan's aggressive behavior was not a "lifestyle" as the personal trainer in LA had forewarned. I felt a burden lifted. Second, her observation restored my confidence in my ability to train Morgan and consequentially allowing me to be less and less afraid of him. My faith had been revived, at least partially, that love-will-conquer all; that with enough love Morgan would be friendly; with enough positive reinforcement he'd behave. Perhaps with abused dogs, such as Morgan, enough love was only half the solution.

So in this case, the two rescued buddies cavorting on the veranda together *was* a miracle, of sorts. When I looked at Morgan my heart filled with love, rather than fear. Morgan was our dog. We were his family, and he was responding. He was changing in another way; he was gaining weight. His face was filling out and appeared more at ease. The calmer he got, the more handsome he became. We had no inkling what Morgan would ultimately look like, never having seen his parents. We observed with amazement as his fur grew longer and curly with hints of beautiful golden hues. I called it his Farrah Fawcett Fur. In the evening as I brushed him, I would say, "Who's the prettiest boy in the world?" He'd make known his answer by the classic Golden smile spread across his face.

The dogs were confined to the porch during dinner. I drew their bones out of the freezer to defrost as we cooked the meal. This was what they'd get while we ate. It felt weird to have to separate my dog from people. Goldens are often the entertainment and the conversation starters. Hopefully, someday, that role would be true for Morgan, as well.

In a customarily manner, our guests arrived at different times. Everyone greeted the pups warmly, visibly appreciative they were safely behind the gate, especially Morgan, as we had cautioned them of his temperament. After people were seated, James rose to express thanks, "I have immense gratitude that Leena thinks Morgan is a changed dog from when we first got him. It's a miracle."

Everyone turned to see Morgan, peering over the porch gate with his new best friend, Wookie. They raised their wine glasses and cheered, "It's a miracle!"

CHAPTER THIRTEEN

I DON'T LIKE SPIDERS OR SNAKES

BY THANKSGIVING TEMPERATURES IN THE DESERT plummeted to more comfy levels. Outdoor activities were back on the schedule. We were on one of our morning hikes in Las Palmas when James mentioned, "The Ukrainian is convinced we ought to have Morgan enrolled in a rattlesnake class and I agree."

Oh no, I thought, shaking my head, let's not do this. I knew James meant Peter, who had the Ridgeback named Ivy.

Rattlesnakes lived out here in the desert southwest. This was their home. When the sun beat down these cold-blooded reptiles slithered out to warm themselves. They rested along the flat surface of trails. The poisonous ones could send a big dog to the hospital. A lot of people worried about snakes. I had never perceived the threat seriously, even as there most likely were several of them living on the very mountain where we stood.

None of my dogs ever had problems with them. The scheme of some snake charmer, who we didn't know, getting near my Morgan was disconcerting and probably a waste of money. When James persisted, I relented, "If you want this to happen then you make the arrangement. I want nothing to do with this snake oil." I didn't hear about his idea again for a while and figured it was just a short-lived whim of his and I was quite relieved.

Until one afternoon, out of the blue, he announced, "The snake-training people are on their way."

"Are you serious?" I questioned, not thrilled by this news. "Don't you think you might have told me sooner?"

He didn't reply.

Just then a white pick-up truck parked outside the house. Our jaws fell when the young, clean-shaven, handsome trainer introduced himself first, as Ty, and then his gorgeous blonde female assistant, as Max(ina). They could easily have hosted a nature series on Animal Planet. Right away I recalled the dog trainer in LA and his diva partner. We were expecting two gruffer guys, or at least a tougher looking, tobacco-chewing type of female assistant. I couldn't imagine what these two modelesque snake trainers were going to do with our boy.

Ty and Max showed James the electric collar he used in the lesson. Right away, I knew I shouldn't have agreed to this. James veered around and asked, "Are you all right with this?"

I wasn't. In a huge way, I felt trapped. I recognized James really wanted this class, so I didn't stand in the way. Still, it didn't mean I was pleased. Reluctantly, I nodded, and the trainer put the collar around Morgan. I felt guilty about abusing him and not sticking up for him. I hated being put in a circumstance like this, choosing between Morgan's safety and James' happiness.

From the rear of their truck, Max lifted two white plastic, industrial tubs, which usually held paint or laundry detergent and lugged them into the backyard. She stationed them off to the side.

James and I scrutinized from the porch, so we wouldn't be a distraction to Morgan. The assistant pulled something out of a pouch wrapped around her waist. It resembled a live snake. Soon after, I realized it was just skin which she laid on the ground. Naturally, Morgan sped over to investigate. Then we heard him yelp and witnessed him leap into the air as the trainer zapped the first electrical shock. I cringed. This was wrong. Too late to stop it. I didn't want to make a scene. I swore then and there to never, ever, do this to Morgan again. Co-parenting a dog can be such a challenge. This was the first time I'd had to do it and if the truth be known, I didn't love it. I appreciated what parents must go through.

Next, the assistant relocated one of the white tubs into the center of the yard, then reached in and lifted out a live baby Diamondback rattler who skated around her gloved hand. I could identify its gold and black colors. My body tensed as she released the reptile onto the ground. Instantaneously, Morgan zipped to it. I couldn't bear to glimpse, and with my eyes closed I heard Morgan shriek and was aware the second shock had hit him. I felt horrible. I was permitting a stranger to abuse my dog. Poor Morgan. And what if that snake got loose? Suppose it escaped into my cactus garden? This was crazy. I didn't know who these people were; or what kind of credentials they actually had. Swiftly, the assistant snatched the snakelet and deposited it back in the plastic tub.

Up till now, there were no words spoken by anyone while things were proceeding. She then lifted the cover of the second tub, out came another diamondback. But this time big and thick and five-foot-long. She held the head of the reptile firmly in her hand. The rattler opened its mouth revealing long narrow venomous fangs.

"Oh no," I grumbled. How could I allow this to happen? This was truly dangerous. Did they have an anti-venom potion? Did they even know how to treat a dog if bitten? All the same, to be honest, I was now spellbound by the whole thing. The serpent charmers had sold their snake oil to us.

Ty instructed one of us to go to the other end of the backyard and summon Morgan. I could barely watch. Maxina arranged the snake on the ground and immediately the rattler raised its head, ready to strike. I couldn't fathom what was happening on our property. James yelled for Morgan. The snake rotated and stared at him. Morgan eyed the serpent and delicately tiptoed around the outer edge of the yard, as far from the rattler as possible. He scurried over to where we were and leaped onto a lounge chair glaring at us as if he were saying, "Get that thing out of my yard NOW!"

With that, lessons were concluded, and the assistant carried the buckets away. "That's it?" I queried, unconvinced. I was promised Morgan would not go near any rattlesnakes. He'd hear the rattle and skedaddle. James and I spent a few minutes hugging Morgan and praising him for his work, then awarded him a treat. I never knew if the training really worked, because we never encountered a snake on our hikes. But I kept to my word. No one ever put an electric collar on Morgan again.

CHAPTER FOURTEEN

IT'S BEGINNING TO LOOK
A LOT LIKE CHRISTMAS

JAMES' CHRISTMAS EVE DINNER, HELD FOR THE past ten years in his apartment in West Hollywood, was a lively affair. Twenty-five, sometimes thirty people crammed into his small one bedroom. The turkey dinner was eaten wherever you could find a spot to sit. I'd been to a couple of them with Willy and always helped decorate the tree and prepare the meal. Dinner was followed by the Secret Santa game, though sometimes dubbed the White Elephant gift exchange. If you've never played Secret Santa, (and I hadn't until I met James), each guest was expected to bring a ten-dollar gift. All gifts were organized in the middle of the room. Numbers were drawn from a hat to determine the order. The game was always quite competitive. When your number was called you could select a gift from the pile or rob a gift from someone who had already chosen one.

After some discussion, James and I decided to move his traditional Christmas Eve dinner out to the desert. This location would enable me to include some of my friends too, so I wouldn't feel alone and out of place, surrounded by James' long-time friends. This also meant I had to get busy decorating the outside of the property. Usually, I had the red outdoor lights strung around the branches of our spectacular, old, gnarly olive tree in the front of the house done by the beginning of November. On Thanksgiving Day all I had to do was flip a switch to launch our holiday light illumination. This year I was late since the election delayed festooning the property.

Our Christmas decorations were stored in the aluminum shed in the backyard. Getting there meant shuffling by Willy's grave. "Hello Willy. It's Christmas time. I'm sorry you aren't here. It's not the same." Nine months had now elapsed since he had crossed. This would be our first Christmas without him. "I miss you, Willy. All the time."

Morgan nudged my leg drawing me out of my memories. Sliding the metal door open, I hauled out several large plastic containers. Morgan smelled them curiously. Then he gingerly stepped inside the shed. "Get out of there. It's all yucky." I swooshed him away. Old sheds can smell musty and be home to lots of spiders and scorpions. This one was also dusty. "Get away."

He stole a page of an old newspaper laying on the ground and scampered off with his pilfered treasure. I watched him tearing it to pieces as I carted the first two boxes into the house. Eyeing me, he lost interest and tailed along. Again, he sniffed the containers. His eyes shifted back from me to the boxes with inquisitiveness about these new creatures in his house.

The next two boxes I knew to be the outdoor lights and headed to the front yard. Morgan remained right behind me. After opening the boxes, I separated strings of lights and casually plopped them on the bench by the door. Morgan grabbed one end and dashed into the house, the lights trailing behind him.

"Morgan, NO." I speedily caught up to him. "No baby. Not these. You could get hurt." I opened his mouth and gently removed the bulb. Okay, first Christmas disaster averted and a lesson learned. One string out at a time. And away from his grasp. A long time had passed since I had to decorate with a puppy.

I plugged in the old lights left on the tree from last year. Two sets were completely out and a third was only half working. I shinnied up the first branch and replaced them with new ones. I viewed Morgan from above, posing on the patio by the front door. His head fixed high, his winning Golden smile shining up at me. His tongue crept out just slightly in the front of his mouth. Not dangling out the side like a crazed rabid animal. There was no drool. No panting wildly. He was tranquil. Morgan the Magnificent. My spirit warmed. Our house was a home again.

In past years, we used to put reindeer antlers on Willy. He'd travel all over town with them on. To the bank. To the coffee shop. Even as I loved Morgan more each day, I missed Willy. I had to cut off reminiscing and pay attention to what I was doing up in the tree, or I'd fall or poke my eyeball out on one of these prickly twisting branches.

James returned home from LA later in the week and we trucked over to the Palm Springs High School to buy a Christmas tree. The annual sale benefits their school band, which is fantastic and we liked to support them since they marched in the Gay Pride parade every year. An added incentive. I'm all for our parades going mainstream. I want more high school bands and floats like in the Macy's and Rose Bowl parades.

"Make sure Morgan doesn't pee on any trees," I warned, driving into the school parking lot.

"Will he do that?" James quizzed.

"Of course he will. It's a tree. Willy peed on a tree once. And that was the tree we brought home."

"How did that happen?"

"You know Willy always roamed free."

"Make sure you hold him tight. I don't want Morgan making this decision. I want the perfect tree," trumpeted James.

I squeezed his lead firmly when we got out of the truck to keep him close at hand.

"What a pretty dog!" a woman at the table blared. "I have a Golden, too."

"This is Morgan. He's a rescue. This is his first Christmas."

"Can he have a treat?"

"He surely can." I don't usually approve of Morgan having treats. Today I relented because I wanted to stay on her good side in case Morgan acted out.

She reached into a jar.

"Morgan, sit." After Morgan sat, he received his reward. "Thank you," I stated to her.

"What a sweet dog," she added.

The compliment was nice to hear and appreciated. She's right, too. Morgan was a good-natured dog. The goal was to nurture this side of him to grow while limiting the aggression. We joked Morgan was a Jekyll & Hyde Golden.

Morgan tugged at the leash with his nose to the ground. His tail wagged back and forth, high in the air. We were so glad to witness this sight because when we first got him, his tail lay between his legs. At first I let him trail blaze the way. But fearing at any minute another dog might arrive, I changed my mind. "Come on, Morgan. Get back here." I gripped the leash taut, and he stayed by my side.

"Which one do you like better?" James wondered, as he held up two trees standing in the parking lot.

"Turn it around," I requested.

James rotated one tree.

"I can't tell. Let me hold them and you look." I commanded Morgan to sit. When he obeyed, I dropped the leash. This was risky. Any moment a dog might loom out of nowhere. Swiftness was necessary.

We agreed on the one to the left and carried our new Christmas tree to the cashier. Sure enough, another car entered with a dog. Time to take refuge. We'd had a fun time and now we needed to vacate the lot. I didn't want Morgan bothering anyone. The two of us parked ourselves on the tailgate of my truck. James gathered up some discarded branches while one of the volunteers cut the trunk of the tree shorter to soak up more water. When Morgan spotted the other dog I heard his low growl. I lightly poked him with my elbow on his shoulder, like two friends might jostle with each other. "Knock it off," I uttered to him.

He quit and glanced at me. I hooked my arm around his head in a head hug. "You don't need to do that."

I didn't hear any further growls. Best friends again.

Our new Christmas Eve tradition would be a much smaller affair. We invited nine friends over for a late afternoon turkey dinner. As our guests showed up, we put Morgan on the back porch with the retractable gate closing him off. When the meal was served, one of his large beef bones to chew materialized, and Morgan gnawed on it throughout the feast. With a smaller group, dinner conversation was more intimate and quieter. With my hearing loss, this was easier for me to comprehend what was being discussed.

After dinner, our next-door neighbors, Bill and Lonny, joined us in the Secret Santa game. Lonny was the woman Morgan bit during the campaign. James was being kind and generous inviting them. One more penchant that I love about him. On the contrary, exactly upon seeing them my stomach tightened. Her shrill voice grated on me. Frankly, I wish James had not welcomed them.

Everyone picked a number out of a hat to dictate the order of choosing a gift for our first Secret Santa in the desert. Once we were away from the dining table near the back porch, Morgan squatted up close to the gate and spied. Undoubtedly, he'd rather be with us in the living room. I made a mental note. The game was tame compared to the backstabbing action in LA, where people stole gifts from each other in an un-Christmassy way. Needless to say, there were twenty-five or thirty highly motivated and egotistical people in those exchanges, contrary to our Palm Springs-mellow, meager eleven.

The game ended snappily, and the guests prepared to leave. As Lonny weaved her way toward Morgan to say goodbye, I attempted to cut her off. I didn't want her near him. Regrettably, our friend Tom distracted me for a moment. All of a sudden, James angrily cried out, "Morgan bit Lonny." I didn't want to believe it until I saw Lonny holding her wrist. I couldn't hide my distaste for them any longer and cried, "He's behind the gate. What did you do to him?" I knew that something like this was going to happen. This was now the second time Morgan had bitten her. More so, I was mad at myself for not preventing the situation. In exasperation, I blurted, "Why did you go near him?"

To which James responded, "She reached over to pet him and he bit her."

"I'm alright," Lonny declared. "Maybe he was mad he wasn't included. Or maybe he just doesn't like me."

The event floored me. I didn't know what to do or say, except to apologize in a more sympathetic, remorseful tone. "I'm sorry for what I said before. I was upset that I couldn't avoid this. I should have. This is my fault. There's no excuse for him to do that. I'm so sorry."

"Don't be sorry. I'm fine."

Privately, I couldn't wait until they were gone. Dogs know. She was right. Morgan didn't like her and there must be a reason. Why did James have to invite them?

When everyone had departed, James, still fuming, angrily challenged me. "What are we going to do? We could be sued. We can't let this happen again."

I agreed and scathingly added, "No more dinner parties." I was being mean.

With a screwed-up face, he insisted, "Morgan doesn't get near people until we put a stop to this. You need to talk to someone about this. Now is the time to train Morgan once and for all to stop this behavior."

I loathed being scolded. "You didn't stop Morgan from biting her, either." He was right, for sure. After a few seconds of silence, in a more conciliatory tone, I resumed, "I promise I'll search for another class."

I had never faced a predicament such as this before. Years ago, when my first Golden, Nicholas, was fourteen, a bunch of us hung out on the stoop of our 17th Street apartment on a rare hot San Francisco afternoon. Nicholas was asleep on the sidewalk. A young woman, striding by, expounded her love of Golden Retrievers. Lacking permission, and before I could prevent her, she bent down and presented her clenched hand out for him to smell. Nicholas just happened to awaken at the same time and was bewildered. He bared his teeth and she scraped her knuckle on one of his worn-down incisors. Even as she was partly at fault for approaching a sleeping animal, I accompanied her to the emergency room and offered to pay the bill. The hospital, as required, reported the incident to the police. A few weeks subsequent, sheriffs turned up at the door to see Nicholas. After discovering how old he was they left and nothing further transpired. Nicholas and I were lucky.

By asking around, I found a class for Morgan which sounded promising, sponsored by the Palm Springs Kennel Club. The instructor was an officer who trained all the local police canines for the county. According to the friend who recommended him, he was old school. Punishment and Reward. Sort of a disciplinarian kind of guy. Maybe this would work, I supposed. However, the class didn't begin until early February and I wasn't sure how James would feel about another month of no training for Morgan. When I explained the situation to James, I was dumbfounded when he said, "That's perfect."

"Perfect? How is that perfect?" I inquired. He always astounded me.

"We got New Years and then the film festival. Then the class. It's perfect timing."

I remembered shaking my head. Everything is perpetually perfect with him. Here I was upset that I had to delay until February. I preferred the class now. Directly after New Years. Indeed, he was right. The Palm Springs International Film Festival was time consuming, lasting for three weeks. And we typically tried to view as many films as possible. This particular year, our film, "Wild About Harry" was premiering. (The making of this film is told in my first book, *A Golden Retriever & His Two Dads*.)

Additionally, James and I were attending the festival's opening Black-Tie Gala Dinner along with the film's director, our friend, Gwen Wynne. We, similar to a lot of the rest of the town, were abuzz with excitement. "Milk" was the film of the year and Sean Penn, the actor portraying Harvey Milk, was in town to accept an award. I looked forward to the possibility of meeting him. Most of the other cast members of "Milk" would also be there, as would be my friend, Cleve Jones, who had started the AIDS Quilt. Cleve was being portrayed by Emile Hirsch.

We had a full house the afternoon of the gala. Our director, Gwen, was staying with us. James hired his friend Tim to come over and make us even more radiant than we already were. Tim was a well-known hair stylist in LA, with clients who regularly contended for Oscars. We were grateful he made time to work at our humble abode for the makeover.

Morgan was relegated to the back porch so he wouldn't distract Tim from his demanding task of transforming us to glow like movie stars. Morgan stalked us from his barrier, with a slight scowl, as Tim cut our hair out on the garden patio on that sunny, mild, early-January afternoon.

That night, as soon as we stepped onto the red carpet with Gwen radiantly dressed in a purple Oscar de la Renta gown and James and I handsomely attired in our black tuxedos, hundreds of reporters from around the world flashed their cameras. We were startled by the attention - until we discovered Emile Hirsch had lined the red carpet right behind us. We all chuckled. So we weren't pursued after by the press; still the red carpet promenade was exhilarating. James introduced Gwen to reporters and camera crews as the director of "Wild About Harry," and some of them did interviews.

Once inside, James was not bashful about introducing himself to people. After we'd met our tablemates (Ron Howard, Tom Bosley, the father in "Happy Days," and Frank Langella star of "Nixon") I took the opportunity to say hello to Cleve. We extended each other a warm embrace and caught up a little. Then he held my arm and introduced me to Sean Penn.

"Thank you for portraying Harvey," I gushed. "It means so much to so many of us."

"It was an honor. Harvey was a great man."

Sean beamed and thanked me when I shared, "I went to all of those demonstrations Harvey led. It felt like I was watching him up on the screen."

"Thank you for saying that. Exactly what an actor wants to hear."

Someone else got Sean's attention, and my moment was over. But I'll have this memory forever. I shook Sean Penn's hand. The man who portrayed my hero. The only detail that could have made this moment better was if Morgan had been with us. My one regret was I didn't get a photograph with him. Regardless, it's forever in my memory. As far as I was concerned, we could leave the gala now. Meeting Clint Eastwood at the after-party was exciting but didn't top this.

Morgan was excited to see us when we returned late that evening. I took him right out for a stroll, still wearing my tux. The stars were brilliant and I could make out the Milky Way along with Mars and Saturn. In that moment, I recollected what all civil rights leaders have understood, namely, change happens slowly, and the struggle continues. My own life had gone from Harvey Milk to marriage equality, from love to loss, to a new home and a new family.

The ensuing night our film premiered at the beautiful Annenberg Theater. When we arrived, there was a line of movie-goers extending up the stairs and around the block hoping to purchase tickets. Canvassing the town with Morgan, passing out postcards announcing the premiere to people we knew (and didn't know) had paid off. Many of the LA crew and cast came out to the desert to see the film, also. They were as giddy and proud as we were to see the turnout. It was a touching reunion and everyone wished to know how Willy was doing.

Each time I took a deep breath to disclose Willy had gotten sick last year, and we had to assist him crossing over. They expressed their condolences and how greatly they had loved Willy. A friend from wardrobe questioned whether I was going to get another one, and I assured her that we already had.

When I shared with her Morgan's photo on my phone, she cried, "Oh! He's adorable. I'm so happy for you."

That night, "Wild About Harry" played to a standing ovation and received a proclamation from the mayor for the film's contribution in the gay civil rights movement. At the conclusion of the festival, while we were home scrutinizing the local evening news, it was broadcast that "Wild About Harry" had won Best of the Fest. James and I jumped up from the couch and hugged each other like they do at the Oscars. Morgan dashed to us and rose on his hind legs to join in the excitement. We each wrapped an arm around him for our first family celebratory moment.

CHAPTER FIFTEEN

THANK YOU, DON JUAN

ON TUESDAY, JANUARY 21, 2009, I AWOKE EARLY and turned on the TV to mark a historic Inauguration Day. President-elect Barack Obama would be sworn in. "Morgan, come on. Up on the bed. I want you to watch this, too," I beckoned to him. He was lying on the floor below on the rug. Morgan sprang up and after some adjusting, he nestled close to me. Having Morgan by my side made me speculate who they would ultimately choose as their "First Dog."

Today was one day I didn't usher him out early. Even in winter, I avoided exposing myself to the desert sun for any length of time. This day, with events starting early from the East Coast, I laid in bed, rubbed his belly, and observed history in the making.

James, back in LA for a few days, and I remained in touch throughout the morning, commenting on the activities occurring on the television in the nation's capital. We were both thrilled with the crowd jamming into the National Mall, which has always had a special space in my core since the AIDS Quilt Inaugural Display there on October 11, 1987. I was part of the crowd of roughly fifteen hundred mourners on that cloudy, cold morning at 7 a.m., when my friend Cleve Jones opened the ceremony. The AIDS Quilt consists of three-by-six-foot individual panels, each one commemorates the life of someone who died of AIDS. The individual panels are sewn into one enormous quilt. One thousand, nine hundred and twenty panels were part of that first display. I had created two of them, with my dear friend Bobby Graham's help. One panel was for my partner, Rick, and a second one for Tim Green, my first boyfriend, the man I travelled to California with back in 1977.

When James returned Friday for the weekend, we practiced training with Morgan, who was not always coming to us when we called his name. So one of us would position himself in the far end of the house and hail for him. Outside, we did the same. Morgan appeared to be grasping the hang of this drill. He was not one hundred percent obedient, but he was coming to us more often.

"Let's go hike the trail behind the museum," James pronounced, on Saturday morning. "Like we used to do with Willy."

"Do you think Morgan is ready?"

"Sure. He comes back when we call him," James asserted.

I wasn't as confident. "Are you sure we're ready?" On this very trail, nearly a year ago, we first learned something was very wrong with our dear Willy. When we reached the top, I thought I heard a boom box playing loud bass. The sound was Willy's breathing. How I hated that day.

"We'll need lots of water. For Morgan, too," I declared.

We packed up peanut butter and jelly sandwiches and several containers of water. This would be a test for all of us. The trail shoots straight up the mountain in a zigzagged pattern. We parked behind the Palm Springs Art Museum and off we went. The first zag led you out of the public area and beyond the driveway of the O'Donnell House, a landmark neo-colonial Mediterranean revival mansion overlooking

O'Donnell Golf Course and the Coachella Valley. It's a "fabulous" location for fundraisers and I rarely use that word. We'd been there just recently for a political soiree.

As we climbed, the muscles in my calves tightened. This day was going to be strenuous, I conceded to myself. Morgan had halted on the trail, panting, gazing down at us as we made our ascent. I prefer my dogs be in front of me on hikes so I could view them, rather than following, where I could possibly not pay as close attention. Step by step, zig by zag, we rose higher. I had to ease up to capture my breath. Already my lungs burned, my chest pounding when I inhaled. "We're out of shape," I voiced, as I gulped for air. "I don't remember it being this difficult." I drew in a breath once more.

James broke off to the side. "A little at a time," he advised in between breaths.

Mesozoic granite jagged boulders that over the years fell from higher points, plastered the mountainside. As we made our way, we were surrounded by broken crumpled metamorphic chunks scattered throughout the path and littering the trail. I turned to assess Morgan just a few feet away from me. His tongue sagged out sideways, akin to when we first got him, which disturbed me a bit. I removed one of the new PBA-free water bottles out of my knapsack and guzzled a big swig. The water tasted good in my parched throat. Then I filled Morgan's collapsible plastic bowl. He slurped up some water. I didn't think he drank enough, "Have some more," I instructed. In an adamant manner, he arched his head away. I gulped more from our bottle and then offered it over to James.

"Ready?" I enquired.

We progressed slow and steady. Sometimes actually slow and unsteady. In prior outings, we'd done this trail in a half hour. We heard voices from below us. Two women sure-stepped their way up the trail seemingly devoid of much effort and eclipsed us without even a nod of acknowledgement. We were too exhausted to be embarrassed or offended. We gained a few more snail steps up. Morgan strode ahead of us. For a third time we paused for a break. I watched Morgan continuing on.

"Morgan, wait," I grunted, expecting him to halt and stare down to us. But he didn't. He continued going. I realized then we had a problem.

"Morgan! Stop! NO!" I shouted. Morgan didn't respond. I staggered as fast as I could up the trail. I didn't know how much farther the top was. I spotted Morgan ahead, close to the two women hikers.

I breathed in deep, struggling for a second wind. It wasn't there. I climbed as diligently as I could, only able to go a short distance. I had to lean over and breathe, letting my hiking stick support me. I felt a bit lightheaded. There wasn't anything I could do. I had to hold off. When I was able, I inched farther. James was below me doing the same thing. I no longer glimpsed Morgan. I recognized he was in that crazed state. The way he would get when we first got him. When he would bark ferociously, irrepressibly at another dog. In this moment I understood Morgan probably didn't know where he was. I teetered up a few more zigzags. At last, I reached the underside of a familiar outcropping of a huge boulder. My recollection was this rock was close to the top.

"Morgan," I could barely talk. "Morgan," I sounded hoarsely. Maybe he'll come back down, I wished. Who was I kidding? Thinking I was close to the highpoint renewed my energy. I hoped he was up there somewhere. Waiting. I prayed he hadn't kept going. My abdomen ached with tightness. My chest throbbed and my lungs stung when I breathed. I put the pain out of my mind.

I observed James a few zigzags below me, resting against his hiking pole. My heart grieved. We overreached, I conceded. Plainly, none of us were prepared for this.

I staggered around the outcropping to discover the trail went higher up. "Shit," I cursed.

Morgan and the women were nowhere in sight. I lurched ahead as rapidly as I could, though not very fast. I persevered, hoping not to stumble. Ultimately, I reached the summit where the trail split in two. One went farther south, higher into the mountain. The other went north and shortly descended down the trail. I didn't view our boy anywhere. Sadness engulfed me. I feared he was gone. Not good in the desert with coyotes so common. Friends of ours had lost their dog on a hike. Now I dreaded a similar fate for Morgan.

"I'm going to go up here and look," I shouted. I bet the bionic women were going on the full trail south. I didn't know whether James heard me.

I forced myself up the path about fifty yards, gasping for my breath, but failed to spy anyone up ahead. Demoralized, I glanced back at James who was waving for me to return. Cautiously, fearful I might fall, I lumbered down to where James was.

He pointed to a picnic table. There underneath, was our boy lying in the only shade anywhere in sight.

My whole body trembled with a sense of relief as I embraced James. "I thought we had lost him." I fought to hold back the tears.

"I know. Me too," James whispered.

My chest was on fire. I hadn't experienced this since running track in high school. I wanted to just slump to the ground right then and there.

Sitting at the picnic table with Morgan at his feet was an old codger with a red bandana wrapped around his head. He reminded me of Don Juan, the character out of Carlos Castaneda's *A Yaqui Way*. The picnic area was a narrow plateau that overlooked the entire Coachella Valley. The panorama stretched from the windmills in the north all the way down to the southern end. On a clear day you could even identify the tip of the Salton Sea, fifty miles away.

I plopped down on the bench. Too tired to acknowledge the old guy. My legs hurt so badly they shook. I massaged them gently to try to get the shaking to stop. Poor Morgan was noticeably exhausted too, lying on the ground panting. He didn't even rise to greet me. His tongue slung low out the side of his mouth, quivering. Even his head was vibrating.

"I thought for certain we lost him," I repeated.

"He came up with the girls. I was sure he wasn't theirs," the old man reported with a chuckle. "I offered him some water and he stayed. I figured someone would be on their way up for him. When I saw your buddy, I said, 'this must be your dog.'"

"Thank God you were here," I uttered, finally able to speak after regaining my breath. "He's a rescue. We've only had him six months. He gets into these frenetic states and acts crazy. He took off with those women. When I shouted for him to stop he acted as if he didn't hear me. I was certain we were past this."

Old "Juan" drank a long swig of water from his canteen. "He's still young. He'll learn."

"We won't be doing this again for a while." James removed lunch from the pack. "We have an extra sandwich," he offered.

"Oh no, thanks. I'm fine. Thank you, kindly." "Juan" turned to face me. "Funny thing, I was just about ready to get up and go on. And something told me to stay a little longer. I always trust my intuition."

"I'm so glad you did," I expressed to him. "You might have saved his life."

"Grateful to have helped. The spirit of the mountain was guarding over him."

We sat in silence as we contemplated his words.

"Juan" stood and stooped down to rub Morgan's head. "Gentlemen. I bid you well."

We watched him head up the Lykken Trail. I rotated to James. "You ready?"

I grasped Morgan's leash and we all rose from the table. Up a mountain may be more exhausting but the downward slope generates a lot more stress on the knees and ankles. I connected Morgan to the leash to make him go slowly as we carefully descended, even though he didn't seem to be in a hurry either. I pivoted back towards the trail to search for the old man and he was nowhere to be found. "James, the old guy has disappeared," I whispered. I don't know why I whispered, maybe out of respect for the mountain spirit.

"No way."

"Ya. I don't see him on the trail."

"I wonder where he went?"

I didn't answer.

We continued our descent. When we paused, James asked, "What happened?"

I understood he meant with Morgan. "I think he went into that crazed frantic state and forgot he was with us."

"Why didn't those women stop?" James deliberated out loud. "They had to know he was behind them."

I shook my head. "Some people won't. Nothing slows them. They're on a mission. You'd have to be dying. And maybe not even then." I relaxed a moment, finally able to admire the panoramic landscape one last time.

"It's a miracle the old guy was there," James expressed.

"For once I agree. It was a miracle. It's like he was there just to save Morgan for us."

"Or was it Willy watching out for us?" James wondered.

There were a few seconds of silence for Willy's memory. We both eyed each other pondering the existence of a Golden Spirit watching out for our boy.

Then he said, "When we get home, I want you to call about that class again. Make sure it's still happening."

CHAPTER SIXTEEN

BOOT CAMP

WALKING THROUGH THE GATE THE FIRST NIGHT OF the training class with the police officer, I shielded Morgan away from everyone else. He sprung out on the leash. "No!" I firmly stated, but Morgan plowed forward. "No!" It was as if I hadn't spoken. He drove again. "No!"

Someone shouted, "How many 'no's' is it going to take?"

Startled, I glanced around, unsure where the words came from. "Me?" I enquired, pointing to myself.

An older, slender man stepped forward and in a loud, condescending manner, demanded, "Which 'no' is the dog supposed to obey?"

I admitted, "I don't know what to do. He's a rescue. He came like this."

I was being made an example, when he scanned around the field and blasted, "One correction. That's all." He marched towards me. I assumed he was the trainer, although he didn't look like your average donut-eating, coffee-addicted police officer. Reaching about five-feet-ten inches tall, he was thin, not more than one hundred and fifty pounds. His hair was short and he had a handlebar mustache. He was dressed in a long-sleeved flannel shirt, pressed blue wrangler jeans and construction boots.

Declaring, "We can't have him attacking other dogs," he held his hand out and asked, "May I?"

I realized he meant the leash and I gladly yielded it over.

He led Morgan toward another dog and when he lunged, the trainer shouted "NO!" and jerked the leash. Morgan flew up into the air and backwards onto the ground.

To see my dog handled in this manner was troubling. Normally, I would never let anyone treat him like this. Then again, I sort of knew what I was getting into. At first, Morgan appeared dumbstruck, but only temporarily. He quickly recovered and stormed towards another dog.

"NO!" the trainer shouted and wrenched the leash. Morgan flew back again, and this time remained sitting, his tongue hanging out; he seemed stunned, no longer interested in charging other dogs. The trainer spun and handed me back the lead. "He won't be going after any more dogs. If he does, that's what I want you to do. You're in charge. Not the dog." As he trooped away, he added, "And you need to have a six-foot leather leash next week."

My turn to be stunned. And relieved. Morgan definitely responded differently. I'd never seen him just sit around a group of dogs like this. As I stood there, Morgan didn't rush at anyone. He didn't thrust forward. Maybe this really was the class for us. This was the "old school" my friend had warned me about. I certainly had gotten personal attention. And I was pleased.

The location for this twelve-week class was a fenced-in, grassy field, which abutted the Palm Springs police station, the very grounds where training for the canine corps occurred. The trainer directed us all to stand on one side along the wall. There were dogs on both sides of us. With great relief, Morgan paid them no mind. In this quiet setting I heard the instructor describe the program, "In each of the coming weeks I'm going to show you a different exercise." Parading back and forth like a general reviewing his troops, he boomed, "We're going to practice right here for a few times. You'll get a chance to ask any questions you might have. Then I'm going to give you all a homework assignment." Staring us down, he threatened, "The following week we'll see who did the assignment and who didn't. If you followed the steps I give you, the dog should be able to do the assignment correctly."

Morgan and I looked at each other shivering in our timbers.

His name was Dan La Master. Sounded made up, like a porn star. He was a chain-smoking retired police officer. A sergeant without the whistle, he coached us to practice heeling this week. "The dog should always be at your left leg. Practice right turns, left turns, about face, fast, slow." He rattled off his orders, "Your dog should pay attention only to you. He follows your lead. You decide where to go and when to go. Not the dog. Right now I want everyone to show me what you're going to do. Let's start out in a clockwise direction."

Morgan and I executed our first exercise perfectly to my relief. After a few rotations the regiment was completed. Several people raised their hands, and he fielded each question.

"How many times a week," one woman asked.

"Until your dog can heel."

"What if I can't get him to listen?" another woman sought to know.

"If you do it the way I showed you, he or she will heel."

I was still a little nervous being so close to fifteen other dogs. I tried to stay calm, worried my feelings may be making Morgan a little anxious, too. Then he humped my leg. "Morgan stop," I said to him as I pushed him down. After a moment he did it again. "Stop," I stated. I didn't want to make a scene. He'd never done this before. I was embarrassed. The good news: he was ardently focused on me and not other dogs.

After class ended, Morgan and I coasted briskly to the truck. I was afraid to socialize, recalling what had transpired at the class in LA, where Morgan had ended up in a scuffle. He vaulted up onto his side in the passenger seat and peered over at me with a wide grin. I truly got the impression he had enjoyed his class. When we arrived home, he hopped out of the truck, whizzed into the house, and camped by the kitchen. Time for his supper.

His exuberance made me smile and melted my affections. This first day of school surely went better than the LA star-driven one. I had found our class. Finally!

Late every afternoon, just as the sun was about to dip behind the mountain, I taught Morgan outside, staying on the streets without traffic. We repeated heeling. Right turns. Left turns. About face. Over and over. The long leash the trainer mandated did help. Already I could see how it gave the dog enough room to scout out mischief and be corrected. Morgan and I devoted about forty minutes every day practicing the lesson Dan La Master had given us for that week.

Wherever I could find a distraction, Morgan and I practiced our next assignment: "sit and stay." At the coffee shop. At our local park. In our neighborhood. When you walked a dog on a regular basis you became familiar with the surrounding streets. You became aware where dogs lived. Where kids lived. Which houses had a lot of coming and going. Before this class, I'd figured what direction to go to avoid these homes. Now these abodes became a destination.

When a dog raced up to the fence to see Morgan, he reacted in his usual snarling hostility, I heaved on his leash, wresting him away like the trainer did. Shouting, "NO!" I hated he did this as much as

I hated having to discipline him. As you would have thought, I never yanked him like La Master did. I just couldn't. Observing Morgan here gave me a glimpse of what must have happened to him in the past. He was probably tied up in a backyard and spent his day barking at the edge of the fence at dogs who passed by. "Fence-fighting" is what it's called. This was the reason, when he did get to play, he wound himself up into a frenzied unruliness and didn't know how to play less hard-hitting. This kind of conduct didn't arise overnight, but was the result of prolonged neglect.

On class night I always got there ahead of time, so we didn't wander into a field full of dogs. This gave us some time to warm up while his schoolmates were showing up. I continued to get the distinct impression he actually liked these classes. He paraded right onto the field and after a few sniffs and lifts, he went into business mode. Like a professional athlete.

Once the lessons started Morgan behaved well, yet he persisted with his habit of springing up on me after each exercise. This behavior soon became obnoxious. I knelt down and patted the ground to get him to finish. The trainer must have caught me bending over, because I heard a voice shout, "Are you going to do that every time you want him to go down?" La Master stomped over towards me. I was a guinea pig again. "I want everyone to watch this." He held the leash in his left hand and said, "Down." Simultaneously, he knelt and with his free hand brought Morgan's front legs forward until his belly touched the ground. La Master barked, "Eventually you won't have to move his legs. Now I want everyone to do it."

When I tried, Morgan was reluctant. "One quick movement," the trainer said to me. I attempted again but Morgan wasn't cooperating. Quite the opposite. He was resisting. Mr. Trainer assured me, "If you keep at it, he'll come around. Guaranteed." Taking a quick look around, I noticed most appeared to be struggling as well.

For the entire week I practiced this exercise with Morgan. Repeating it over and over again. He consistently balked without going down on my instruction. His stubbornness was irritating and my patience was waning. I couldn't understand his resistance, even if this was the most submissive position.

Before training one day we dropped into Koffi for an iced tea. We seated ourselves in the covered cave-like alcove on the side of the building. A couple of gentlemen promenaded by with two Standard Poodles. Morgan sprung and roared. The noise ricocheted off the cement walls and amplified. I grabbed the leash and towed him back. "No! Morgan, down!" Directly, Morgan lay down.

The poodles and their owners moseyed on, away from us. The men shook their heads in what I interpreted as disdain and judgment. I was disappointed Morgan had acted inappropriately again. Especially after all that toil. I presumed we had this contentiousness under control. I was mistaken. I slouched back in my chair and inhaled deeply several breaths. I confess, these interactions always jolted me, impacting my entire body. As I relaxed, I viewed Morgan on the ground. Which meant he went down. MORGAN WENT DOWN!

This was a lesson for me, too. We'd just had a major breakthrough and I hadn't even witnessed it. I was so bothered by other people's opinions I failed to see our own accomplishment. I vowed then and there I would never be embarrassed by Morgan's actions again. I wasn't going to react to other people. Both Morgan and I were grinding hard and doing the best we could. I would always focus on our amazing progress. As the song says, "We've only just begun." I gave Morgan a big hug and said to him, "What a good boy you are."

At obedience class we were now being taught to make our dogs come to us on command. We maintained the dogs on leash as we paced through our warm-up routine. Morgan trotted ahead of me, and

I tugged him back and suddenly heard, "Why is the Golden ahead of you? Pulling him back on the leash will only make things worse."

I was in trouble again. The trainer barged towards me. A foot away, like a drill sergeant, he loudly declared, "If you were more consistent with your corrections, that dog would behave right all the time."

As usual, I didn't enjoy being singled out and scolded in this manner. I didn't believe his reaction was warranted for such a minor infraction. I was giving everything I had into this training, which wasn't always easy. This guy didn't know, nor maybe even care that my standing there for an hour every Tuesday night caused my feet and legs to ache from my neuropathy. Right then, my decision to just keep my mouth shut and not create trouble seemed the best course of action. For Morgan's sake, I would not let this get personal. This guy had taken us so far. I truly trusted he wanted Morgan to learn to obey so he could have a good life. At least at this training class I was getting personal attention, unlike the celebrity-focused trainer in LA. This kind of class was not for everyone. One guy who I was acquainted with, stormed off the field after he had this kind of interaction with La Master trainer and never came back. That was not going to happen to us. I also noticed he only yelled at the guys. Never the women. I suspected he was using me and Morgan as a teaching example for the class.

The rest of that evening was uneventful compared to the start. Morgan aced his task to "come." It gave me satisfaction to have Morgan behave well. This upcoming week's assignment was a breeze.

Then it was time for the "sit and stay" off leash. We trained all week at the neighborhood park where there were kids and dogs, joggers and bicyclists. We were instructed to prepare with distractions around. Morgan completed perfectly. I was confident he had this exercise in the bag, as they say. That week's class, when we were doing the "sit and stay," La Master took out a tennis ball and tossed it. When the ball rolled by Morgan he broke after it. I caught up to him, with the ball in his mouth. I heard everyone laughing. Even La Master was chuckling, the only time I ever saw him laugh. Morgan was so proud to retrieve the ball. I couldn't help myself, either. I just shook my head. I mean, really, it was such a cliché. Naturally the Golden chased the ball!

Morgan's graduation from training class was just before Easter. The test was qualifying in a dog competition routine using the same drills we'd been rehearsing the previous twelve weeks. Participants in class invited friends and family to delight in the final assessment. I actually asked for James *not* to come. Morgan didn't need any extra distractions. Though in hindsight I wish that he had. La Master wasn't on the field for the test class which was all very official and conducted by a woman from the Palm Springs Kennel Club. Each owner got a checklist of exercises to perform which would be scored. The obedience official explained that one hundred total points was a perfect score. A passing score was seventy-five.

One at a time, the owners were requested to bring their canines out to the center of the field, to go through the routine. When our name was called, Morgan started out well, doing a perfect "heel and about face" and "sit." When we progressed to the off-leash portion of the test, Morgan mounted me and humped my leg. Then he squatted in front of me with a huge grin on his face making me think the joke was on me. As though he had been anticipating the entire length of the training to do just this. When we performed the required figure 8s, off leash, Morgan decided he was doing figure 6s and took off to pee in the bushes without closing the final loop. I had to catch him and fetch him back to finish.

When the time came for the final exercise, to call the dog to come, which was worth twenty-five points, nearly a third of the test, Morgan posed perfectly still. When I called, "Come Morgan." He took five paces forward as I held my breath. Halfway through, Morgan bounded about the field like a kangaroo. Then he twirled around, rolled on his back, and wiggled in the grass like dogs do when they're happy. The other owners were hooting. Even the judge chuckled. When I pursued him before any trouble developed, he sprang up and scampered to the back of the field. He was obviously enjoying his game of tag. This back and forth lasted a few more minutes until the judge in a playful voice, said, "Morgan, come to me." He trotted over to her, where I could leash him. People clapped at the performance and I just shook my head and said, "That's my boy." And I loved him even more that day.

Understandably, we didn't pass. When the judge calculated Morgan's scorecard, his total was a whopping thirty points. I smiled. I wasn't disappointed because together we had completed the class. Morgan and I were bonding on an important level. Twelve weeks around other dogs and not one fight; not one incident. And he loved coming to class. I could tell by the way he proudly headed onto the field beforehand and then jumped into the truck after each week, like a young kid finishing his Little League game. Before we walked away, the official said to me, "You have a good dog. He's funny. I hope you keep up the training with him." Then she shared, "I can't pass Morgan, but have the discretion to give him a Good Neighbor certificate. Congratulations."

CHAPTER SEVENTEEN

HIS OWN OCEAN BEACH STORY

AT THE END OF APRIL, WE PACKED THE TRUCK AND steered north. Another film produced by James, *Kimjongilia*, about the children's concentration camps in North Korea, was in the San Francisco International Film Festival. James and I had made the nine-hour trip there twice before with Willy. This would be the first one with Morgan. The weather called for showers off and on all weekend which was welcome news. Living in the desert, we missed the rain even in the winter. Average yearly rainfall is only five inches. In April a scant .008 inches is normal.

Gloriously, the weather was stormy when we awoke the first morning in San Francisco. We reached the beach at noon to find a deserted paradise, empty except for seabirds and surfers. We trudged through the sand down to the shore. I commanded Morgan to sit, and then, as if I were checking both ways before crossing a busy street, I scanned the beach one more time before letting him loose. There was no one in sight. Morgan dashed out into the surf. He hopped and bounced from side to side. I threw a tennis ball out into the water and he leaped out above the surf to find it. Then he eyed a seagull gliding just above the waves. He galloped after the bird full-speed-ahead. Like a thoroughbred. I marveled at his swiftness and agility. He was breathtaking. A thing of beauty.

The gull flew farther along, always remaining above the water, until he angled out into the surf. Morgan was relentless and prolonged his pursuit until the water became deep enough to impede his progress and he halted. After a moment he turned and stared at us, as if wondering: what now?

I beckoned him back to shore, but he didn't respond. He remained gazing out into the ocean. We didn't see anything except for a lone surfer sloshing out behind his board. Morgan tore out, hurdling over the incoming waves. James wasn't sure what our boy was doing, and I pointed, "He's going out to that surfer."

"This isn't good," James declared.

"Morgan! MORGAN!" we both shouted.

The surfer paddled farther out. A whitecap washed over our dog and he pierced right through it. Morgan was no longer fearful of the ocean or the waves, like he was back in September at the beach in Malibu. James and I both yelled frantically for him to come back as he was now up to his chest. Luckily, the surfer figured out what Morgan was doing and caught the next wave in to shore. Morgan accompanied him in, and I waved a thank you. Our dog bounded up out of the ocean and strolled over to us. He was soaked and water dripped from his fur, giving him that seal-like quality for which Goldens are famous. I hadn't seen Morgan look like this before. Just then a flock of small shore birds swung by overhead, and Morgan was off again, sprinting into the water. The birds flew on with Morgan tailing.

After about a half hour the rain fell harder. Time for us to head back. I spied Morgan ahead of us on the beach, sniffing at something in the sand. "I hope he doesn't get into anything," I said, thinking a clump of seaweed. Or a dead bird. Then I perceived whatever he was occupied with, stir. "Oh no. That's an animal." I sprinted to Morgan as fast as I could and coerced him away. There in the sand was a small harbor seal. He appeared sick. Upon closer inspection, I noticed he had an open wound on his side, as if he'd been shot. The poor animal had closed his eyes.

"We can't leave him like this. We need to contact the Marine Mammal Center," I hollered to James, a few yards behind me. I had visited the center in Marin once before. I dialed the number and reported the situation. A volunteer informed me someone would be there within thirty minutes.

We waited a safe distance from the injured seal. Soon a guy dragging a large kennel and butterfly net emerged on the beach. We pointed him to the animal. He draped the net over and around the seal, and then coaxed the pup into the kennel. Once he had the animal safely secured, we helped haul the crate up the sand and into the back of his truck. James wondered if the poor guy would be all right. The volunteer disclosed to us, "This was the third we've rescued in a week. The others are recovering, so he should, too." He added, "Good thing you found him and called, as he might have been there all day and night in weather like this. Then he asked, "What do you want to name the seal? Since you found him, you get to name him."

"Actually, our dog found him. We were way over there," I answered, pointing. I thought for a moment, then declared, "Let's name him Morgan. He rescued him."

The volunteer patted Morgan on the head and told him, "Good job!"

Before Morgan, I had always hoped to rescue an injured animal like the seal. In reality, what are the chances of this occurring? Unmistakably, our lives with this crazy misfit would never become dull. Our very own Jekyll & Hyde Golden. Our modern-day terror-dactyl.

I never imagined that our wild boy Morgan would make it come true. Our rescued boy was now a rescuer.

I kept my hero on a leash as we shuffled through the wet sand away from the rescue site just in case he had any crazy thoughts of returning to the spot. The rain continued falling and I wouldn't have wanted it any other way. Ocean Beach. I couldn't believe I was here once again with my dog. It felt like I had grown up here. I was nineteen when I first moved to San Francisco. I spent many years coming out here with my previous two Goldens. We had so many adventures, from one end of the beach to the other. I chuckled when I realized Morgan now had his own Ocean Beach story to tell.

CHAPTER EIGHTEEN

TIME AFTER TIME

ALMOST A YEAR AFTER WE RESCUED MORGAN I observed a real change in his behavior. One night, James was away and I was alone in bed with Morgan lying next to me. I removed my hearing aids and could literally hear nothing. He suddenly held his head tall and perfectly still, with a serious expression on his face. His movements surprised me but also pleased me. I recognized instantly what was happening, and I watched to see what he did next. His ears twitched back, and he moved his head slightly to the left. I couldn't hear anything, but he must have. Some cats or the fruit rats next door. I doubted there was a prowler, but you never know. I slid down next to him and whispered, "What a good boy you are." Off and on over the next hour he repeated his actions.

In the morning I learned from Bonnie, our next-door neighbor, that some cats had been screeching and fighting and keeping her awake. She confirmed what I suspected: Morgan had begun to protect his home. He was being my ears. I could now count on him to tell me if there was anything going on around the house or outside.

A few months later, we had another encouraging breakthrough. Morgan popped into the bedroom and stood by my desk staring at me. At first his demeanor seemed odd, but cute. I thought he wanted to play, then it dawned on me that perhaps someone was at the house. Grabbing my hearing aids, I opened the front door to find a package delivered for me. I remembered how touched I was when Nicholas and Willy had first demonstrated this skill. They had aced this task much earlier. Everything took longer with Morgan. Abused animals are at such a disadvantage. I rubbed Morgan's head in appreciation knowing I was being safeguarded again.

I have always enjoyed hiking with my dogs. When my first partner died, I would escape with Nicholas to my friend Phil's four-thousand-acre ranch in Sonoma County, which brought me tremendous solace. In Palm Springs, Willy and I began to explore all the local trails. But sadly, he passed away before we became more serious about hiking.

With Morgan, I hiked farther than I had ever gone before. He clearly loved scurrying up the switchbacks and pulling me along with him. I always needed to keep closer tabs on Morgan than I had with Nicholas and Willy. Making sure he was safe and rested. I even bought new, sturdier hiking boots and a wooden walking stick for myself. I packed lunches and snacks and plenty of water for Morgan and me. Together, we crisscrossed the narrow rocky "goat trails" at the south end of town that begin behind the Vons market shopping plaza. They're called goat trails because bighorn sheep travel along these paths to graze in winter.

We could go from one end of the ridge to the other overlooking Araby Cove and south Palm Springs, which was a strenuous three-mile trek. Morgan and I would take a breather and relish some sliced organic apples while taking in the awesome view. By the way he was surveying the panorama, then glancing over at me, I had the distinct impression that Morgan was admiring the vista as much as I was. His expression made the arduous effort all worthwhile.

Without a doubt, we were growing stronger together. Morgan's thin body had turned into a muscular athletic machine. We were ready for an adventure up to the Skyline Trail which veers straight up the mountain, reaching a three-thousand-foot elevation. From this vantage point we overlooked the entire Coachella Valley. We discovered that there's a permanent first aid box at the top of the trail complete with tape, bandages and even a couple of small bottles of water. We celebrated our achievement with Morgan's favorite peanut butter and jelly sandwiches. James snapped a memorable picture of Morgan and me that looks like I was a sheep herder with his trusted dog in the dry mountains of Crete, complete with my walking stick/shepherd's staff. These accomplishments lifted my spirits. We had a new identity – HIKERS!

I became obsessed, like Forrest Gump with his running. Hiking became more important to me than anything else. However, the long outings inflamed my neuropathy in both my legs and feet. I was slow to rise the next day so we would take a break, but only for a day. Usually, by the following morning, we went right back out. Into the wilderness. Morgan was always eager and ready for another trail adventure.

When Morgan was about six, I was confident that all of his consistent training had paid off. He was now a well-behaved dog. The time had arrived to apply for his service dog license from the Palm Springs Animal Control. I used the same plan as when I secured a license for Willy. First, I obtained a letter from my HIV doctor and then one from my ear doctor, both describing the services that a hearing dog can assist me with. His tag permitted us to go everywhere together. Restaurants, department stores, parks and hospitals. And yes, even onto a plane so he could begin to travel "Back East" with me. I was so relieved when Morgan was awarded his official service dog license. Together, we went out to celebrate at Tyler's Burgers in downtown Palm Springs with a burger for each of us, along with some thick fries.

With his official license and service cape, I was allowed to take Morgan on the Palm Springs Aerial Tramway which travelled from the floor of the Coachella Valley to the base of the summit of Mt. San Jacinto. The tram cars rotate slowly, offering spectacular vistas of the surrounding mountains and the vast desert below. Morgan handled the trip like a pro, even when the tram car swung back and forth crossing the towers that hold the cables. He looked up at me and grinned as most of the other tram riders gasped. Leaning forward, I mouthed to him, "That's my boy."

The car landed at the Mountain Station and the doors swooshed open. Morgan rushed out onto the platform with me holding firm to the long leash. He led the way along the corridor, down the wide staircase and out into the park forest, as though he could smell the fresh pine air and knew where to go. I loved his gusto and just let him lead the way.

Initially, we stayed in Long Valley, close to the tram station. At this eighty-five-hundred-foot elevation breathing can be difficult when doing strenuous exercise, and I wanted to see how the thin air impacted Morgan. This is where most visitors explored. After a few trips, I could tell he was ready for something more invigorating, so we ventured farther to the Ranger Station. The more skilled hikers congregated in this area before they began their ascent to the peak. To advance into the wilderness, a day permit was required to be completed by each individual.

I loved filling out the permit, which always boosted my mood. No matter what was happening in my life, being in the great outdoors was where I could let go of my frustrations with the multitude of medical conditions I faced. This was my meditation. I loved being there with Morgan. There's a box on the form that asked how many were in your party. Writing down Morgan's name as my service dog always evoked a smile. I loved watching him follow me around boulders up to the higher elevations.

In all our years of hiking, I saw only one other dog at that height. A small lap dog. The law states that all dogs remain on a leash. I have to admit, as soon as we proceeded on past the Ranger Station, I let Morgan free. He understood to stay close to me. At this elevation you didn't bump into too many other hikers. But if I heard any voices coming in our direction, I leashed him quickly.

Mt. San Jacinto State Park was our oasis in the hot months, enabling Morgan and I to escape the heat. The desert floor roasts at 110 degrees, but within twenty minutes we were on the tram to the top where the temperature was a comfortable 75 degrees. We've been there during each and every month, in rain, snow, sleet and hail. In the winter, if snow had fallen the previous night, we could be the first people in the park the next day. Morgan loved running and rolling in the snow. I dressed him in silly winter hats and captured pictures.

As with Willy, the biggest test for Morgan as a certified service dog transpired on his first plane ride to Cape Cod. Officer Dan La Master's training had paid off. When I fastened the official orange service cape around Morgan, he became serious, or knew enough that he was *supposed* to be serious. Our check-in at the Palm Springs International Airport went smoothly. But the challenge rose with TSA. They mandated that Morgan go through the metal detector on his own. This rule made me extremely nervous until I saw Nathan, a friend of mine from the gym, working at the X-ray gate. We greeted each other with smiles. He instructed James to hold back Morgan while I went through the metal detector. Then I called him to come from the other side of the gate. He ran through into my arms wiggling, receiving a round of applause from the patient travelers behind us. Boarding was equally as smooth until the flight attendant reached out to pet him and then held back after seeing the "Do Not Pet" patch on his orange cape. "I'm sorry. I'm not supposed to do that. I can't help myself."

I smiled. "That's okay, you can pet him," I said, knowing it was wise to have a strategic ally in case Morgan acted up on the plane.

Relieved that we had boarded without any problems, James and I fell asleep once the flight stabilized but soon awoke to the sound of laughter. Morgan had crawled under the seats in front of us, determined to meet a fellow travel mate, a white Bichon, three rows in front of us. The entire plane was laughing. Even the flight attendants were chuckling and shooting pictures with their cell phones. As I've said before, Goldens get away with so much more than other dogs.

However, one of Morgan's biggest breakthroughs occurred when our friend Leo brought home a cream-colored Golden Retriever puppy named Cody. We took them up to Whitewater Preserve for an outing when Cody was small and young. Morgan tried to play roughhouse but I closely monitored his behavior so there was never any problems. As a result Cody was never afraid of Morgan. He grew up with him. Before long, Cody's head was huge, and he towered over Morgan. We hung out at the back of the grassy knoll at Koffi. The two dogs rolled in the lawn barking at each other. To see Morgan finally have a BFF caused me immense joy. He wasn't less rowdy with Cody, but he was so big that when Morgan grabbed his neck all he got was a mouthful of fur. After their rambunctious rumbles in the turf, the two of them sat together, panting.

Eventually, Leo trusted us enough to take Cody on our hikes. When we picked him up, Cody sped out of his house and hurdled into our car. The two dogs started barking straightaway like boys talking about sports or their latest crushes. These adventures always began with a loud wild ruckus of tumbling in the dirt. But by the time we headed home, they were strolling together as though they were chatting about how much fun they had had. Cody shook things up, and we loved his big tenderhearted polar bear head.

A few years back, in 2016, I had an unexpected development when I went back for a checkup with my old ear doctor, Dr. Schindler, in San Francisco. Not five minutes into the appointment he said, "Why don't we close up that hole now?"

He was referring to the perforated ear drum in my right ear. I'd been waiting for those words for a long time. I flashed back to that day in 1989 when he said to me, "Someday when your ears are dry, and your immune system is better we'll patch up that hole in your ear drum."

At the time, I wondered if he were just being kind. I never expected to live long enough for this procedure to occur. "You really think so?" I asked him.

"Yes, I do. What are we waiting for? Until you're seventy?" he joked. (I was fifty-seven when he spoke these words to me.) "Let's do it now."

The surgery happened without any complications. The only thing that hurt was the area behind my ear where the skin had been taken for the graft. A few months after, a new test confirmed that hearing in my right ear had improved, even though I was still considered hard-of-hearing.

Back home in Palm Springs, we dropped in on a friend who had a pool. With some hesitation I dove in for my first swim without my ear plugs. Such freedom not to have to wear them! But when you've had a hole in your ear drum for as long as I did, I have to admit, I was apprehensive afterwards. That night I heard gurgling and some rumbling in my ear. I ruminated if water had seeped in. I feared an infection might develop so I made an appointment with my local ear doctor to have him check me out. He said, "Your ear looks fine. The graft is holding. Stop worrying." A few weeks later we were back in San

Francisco, and Dr. Schindler said, "The graft looks great. You're fine. Stop worrying."

Certainly, I felt relieved. But to stop worrying? That's impossible for someone like me who has lived with HIV my entire adult life. How could I not be doubtful? The AIDS epidemic is not over. People are still dying from complications of this disease.

The only time I ever ceased fretting; the only time I felt peace; the only time I felt a spiritual comfort was with Morgan high up in the mountains far away from people. Hiking up on the mountains was my version of a veteran coming home after the war and hitting the road on a Harley Davidson.

When you've spent so much of your time battling an epidemic, the survivors never fully recover. I'm always told that I'm one of the lucky ones, but honestly, I don't always believe that. When I'm around people I don't know, I tend to get quiet. I don't want to recount my history to anyone. Even within the gay community, a place where I might get support, I can feel disconnected. The new generation hasn't gone through what we went through. They don't seem to understand. But then how could they? I don't talk about knowing Harvey Milk. I don't talk about the AIDS epidemic. I'm like one of those people who have had their past stricken from their file.

When Morgan was the grand old age of eleven, you would think that he would have settled down into this mellow ol' grandpa enjoying his stature. Not so. He remained as feisty as ever, preserving the reputation of his namesake, Captain Morgan the Pirate. When we visited our friend Ken in Santa Barbara, who has two Basenjis, Skyler and Charlotte, his mischievous self emerged in seconds. We'd been before, so Morgan was familiar with the layout. Upon greeting, he darted right inside Ken's apartment and stole Skyler's favorite stuffed toy, causing a huge ruckus within minutes.

When Morgan first joined our family, I was concerned that I would have to forego my political work because he required constant supervision and training. On the contrary, he has inspired me to apply my political skills to the rights of animals. To end the slaughter of dogs in Asia. To halt the decimation of animal life on the planet. And locally, the banning of toxic pesticides in our local park where Morgan and I strolled each morning.

Our companions never live long enough. As Morgan aged, I worried about losing my boy and what life would be like without him. But no good comes from dwelling on what will happen, or *might* happen. Whenever those anxieties surfaced, I'd hug Morgan tight and then hug him some more. I'd tell him I loved him and then tell him again.

You just could never let your guard down with him, ever, even at age twelve. But that is what I have loved about our years with Morgan. The unexpected. The excitement. And Morgan's incredible love for adventure. As senior citizens, Morgan and I would participate in a bedtime ritual together. We each took our own glucosamine pills for our joint ailments. We both had anti-inflammatory meds for our knees and hips. And both of us actually shared the same eye drops for our eyes. Oddly enough, he loved taking his pills. I wish I had his enthusiasm. But this same unrelenting fervor motivated us out the door for our early morning loop around the park that had replaced our challenging vigorous mountain hikes.

I am amazed by how much more I notice when we go slowly. And with my ear repaired and my new more powerful hearing aids, how much more I can hear. Before the operation I had not heard the flutter of hummingbird wings in over thirty years. Most recently, I witnessed a symphony of a tapping woodpecker on an old fir tree.

One afternoon, as COVID was about to descend on America, we ambled along the golf course in Palm Springs. When we returned home, Morgan laid down on the kitchen floor and didn't move. He didn't even try to get up. The incident had no explanation. He had been moving fine that morning. For five days this went on. He was now thirteen. We decided not to do any heroic procedures or treatment. We even made arrangements for our vet to come to the house if Morgan didn't improve.

Sunday evening is a day reserved for pasta in our home. I was cooking dinner so the aroma of garlic and onions and oregano wafted throughout the condo. When I peeked over at Morgan, he had raised his head off the floor. He must have been enticed by the fragrance of my Italian cuisine. Dinner that night was a cause for celebration.

Saying goodbye to Morgan was postponed. Still, he may have been present and alert, but he couldn't walk on his own. We weren't sure what to do. After discussing the situation with some close friends, we resolved to buy a red Radio Flyer wagon to transport him around. Morgan was still a happy boy, his smile as wide as ever. Thus began the era known as the "wagon-walks." Because of COVID the golf course was shut, allowing us to haul Morgan in his wagon around the eighteen holes on the cart path twice a day, early morning and again after the sun set. People living along the fairways would wave to us and shout, "Hello, Morgan. Are you enjoying your walk?" He'd flash his wide smile at them. Sometimes offering a bark.

We spent most of COVID sheltered in Palm Springs for over a year. During this time, we concluded our days in California were ending. We really wanted to be near our nieces and nephew on the East Coast. In December 2020, still under lockdown, we purchased a cottage in the small town of Buzzards Bay, Massachusetts, a block from the beach.

Every day I was troubled with the prospect that Morgan might not live long enough to make the trip across the country to our new home. The thought of burying him on the West Coast and leaving him behind was unbearable. I didn't know if I could realistically do that.

But with pure grace he held on. We celebrated late April 2021 the publication of my book, *A Golden Retriever & His Two Dads*, and the fact that Morgan was well enough to travel with us to Cape Cod, much to my relief. A month later, on May 17, at ten a.m., James and I bid our farewell to California and motored east. Both of us having lived there for forty-five years.

Our journey across the country was slow and steady, stopping to visit historic sites. Morgan paid tribute at the solemn Lincoln Tomb in Springfield, Illinois. The weather was perfect the entire trip. Just a shower here and there. On May 27, at 3:30 p.m. we wheeled into the driveway of our new yellow Cape Cod home. Once on the lawn Morgan rolled onto his back and seemed delighted to be out of the car and probably grateful the trip was over. We, however, were daunted by the unpacking that now lay ahead of us.

A few days after our arrival we hauled Morgan in his red wagon down to the beach. Together, we carried him into the bay to cool him off. We were amazed when he suddenly moved his legs freely. Swimming was something he always loved to do. Then one day it dawned on me. Why don't I get him a life preserver to help him stay above the water? The next day he swam on his own. He even retrieved his tennis ball. To see his old self re-emerge was so heartening.

It didn't take long for the neighbors to approach and welcome us. Many were touched by our love for Morgan. When not swimming, we were busy un-boxing clothes and kitchen appliances, hurrying out to buy plants and cleaning supplies and arranging furniture and art work. As well as spending time in the yard with Morgan.

During the summer and fall 2021 we stole time outs to visit Provincetown and sell my book at bookstores across Cape Cod. Morgan was an expert salesperson. When folks came over to greet him, I made my sales pitch. Morgan was a happy boy and people loved to meet him and have pictures taken. But around Christmas time, Morgan's health slipped. He could no longer hold his head up on his own. We recognized that the end was approaching. From then on, we would keep him comfortable. The neighbors provided us with the name and number of a mobile vet. She came to the house to check on Morgan and prescribed us a sedative if we found that he was in pain.

Once more, he perked up and held his head high. But this time was different. On the morning of February 11, Morgan, who always had a hearty appetite, stopped eating. We foresaw something had changed and the end was upon us. His breathing became shallow. That evening, we laid him in bed with me and I held him close. I calmly and softly expressed goodbye to him and thanked him for our amazing life together. He stared at me with glassy eyes, and I sensed he was saying goodbye, that he was thanking me for giving him that same special life. At 3 a.m., February 12, 2022, Morgan took his last breath.

At first there was a feeling of relief that Morgan was free from his exhausted body and that we no longer had to pick him up. We buried him in the back yard near a rhododendron bush. James burned incense, and I lit white candles to honor him and to guide his journey. But after a couple of days of sleep and quiet, the realization that he was never coming back crept in. Grief descended on me as I considered all the things we would never do again. Little things like taking a walk. Or tossing a tennis ball. Most of all, I missed touching him and reciting to him he was "the prettiest boy in the whole world." I felt devastated. This grief felt worse than the loss of my first two Goldens. But I knew that wasn't true. Each loss was a tremendous blow. Each time losing my best friend.

Morgan had such a rough start. He came to us aggressive, abused, and undernourished. Without a doubt, raising him was more challenging than my first two Goldens. But as Auntie Mame once said, "Life is a banquet and most poor suckers are starving to death." Despite the rocky start, our life was definitely a banquet, on both land and sea. What other dog can say he swam in San Francisco Bay with a backdrop of the Golden Gate Bridge, the Pacific Ocean in Malibu, the Gulf of Mexico in Naples, Rehoboth Beach on the Atlantic while a school of porpoise leaped by, Maine, Cape Cod, and lastly our own Buttermilk Bay? What other dog can claim to have hiked on the Pacific Crest Trail in Palm Springs and Franklin Canyon Park in Beverly Hills, overlooking the Pacific Ocean? Or walked in the Rachel Carson National Wildlife Refuge and camped in Acadia National Park? A banquet, indeed.

Throughout his life, Morgan taught me so many things. First and foremost, *he taught me how to be more patient.* An abused dog takes extra time to learn the basic socialization skills. *He granted me a refresher course on compassion.* My heart reached out to him each time I thought about the abuse he endured before coming into my life. There was *the constant forgiveness for his mistakes and for mine.* Trusting that we were both doing the best we could. And of course, I'll always remember that day at the private trainer's shop, when I had to decide if I wanted to commit to the work that an aggressive Golden would demand. I looked down at Morgan sitting by my side. He gazed up at me with his lovable face. I reached down and petted his head and vowed: yes, I would set aside my hearing problems and my other health concerns and would pledge to give Morgan the life every young dog deserves. And that's the life he lived.

EPILOGUE:
A NEW BEGINNING

IN THE FIRST WEEK OF MARCH 2022, MY FRIEND LISA in Florida sent me a picture of a 6 year-old, cream-colored Golden Retriever named Franklin, who needed a forever home. Her email read, "What do you think of Franklin?"

Just the name Franklin made both of us smile, sounding so East Coast New England. As though he belonged at Yale or Amherst College. James was immediately on board with welcoming Franklin into our home. Me, not so quickly. I wasn't ready. Only three weeks had passed. My mourning had barely begun. My heart was still fractured. I wanted Morgan back. I didn't want to forget him or replace him.

But there was something about Franklin besides his name. He looked like our old friend Cody. So we felt like we knew him already, like he belonged with us. After a couple of days my resistance lessened. We knew that there weren't many Goldens to rescue. Just thinking about a puppy in the house exhausted us. I came to the realization that if we didn't act quickly on Franklin, he would be lost to us.

On March 23, our friend Lisa arrived at our home. This giant ninety-five pound ball of fur named Franklin jumped out the back seat of her SUV, ran into the house through the side door, and settled in, declaring he was home. And you know what? We all felt the same way. Even though my heart ached, I knew Franklin belonged with us.

Franklin is big in a lot of ways. Big head. Big paws. And most importantly, a big heart. That's what has won us over. Morgan's passing was still recent and raw, but Franklin was helping my heart to mend and to open again. I leave you with this poem I discovered:

It came to me

that every time

I lose a dog

they take a piece

Of my heart with them,

And every new dog

who comes into my life

gifts me with a piece

of their heart.

If I live long enough

all the components

of my heart

will be dog, and

I will become as generous and

as loving as they are.

—Anonymous

Franklin is now the face of *A Golden Retriever & His Two Dads* and *Rescuing Morgan*. But my next book will be called *Everyone Loves Franklin*. And it's true. Nearly everyone we meet falls instantly in love with him. You will, too.

ACKNOWLEDGEMENTS

I want to take this opportunity to thank all of the different people who have edited my work over the years: Barbara Kuhl, Steven Simmons, NC Heikin, Jerry Roscoe, Bill Ferrall, Sherry Burke, Courtney Perdios. I have been extremely fortunate to have these writers and friends with me on my writing journey. Ongoing editing has remained the work of my friend and former poet laureate of West Hollywood, Charles Flowers and my hubby James Egan, who has been a day-to-day witness to my constant bouts of insecurity and frustration and shared my joy with the final manuscript.

Once again, many thanks to Al Mueller for the cover photo of both *Rescuing Morgan* and my first book, *A Golden Retriever & His Two Dads*. And to Scott A. Beyer in Vermont for his steadfast and crucial technical support. He's kept my website going and growing.

To dog trainer Officer Dan La Master for always being a "tough bastard" with me and drilling into my brain: "If you were more consistent with your corrections, that dog would behave right all the time."

To our good friend Leena Deneroff for her early support and advice on training Morgan. And, of course, to Casey Criste for his open-door policy to his resort for all those fun years.

To Leo Newcomb for letting us borrow his beautiful Golden boy Cody for trips around the Greater Palm Springs area and for becoming Morgan's BFF.

ABOUT THE AUTHOR

Dan Perdios has been fortunate enough to be rescued by four Golden Retrievers. Willy, the co-star of his first book, *A Golden Retriever & His Two Dads*, was a light blond puppy with bright gold eyes and arrived in 1996, after his first Golden, Nicholas, passed.

Dan is an extensively published, PEN Grant award-winning journalist. His articles have appeared in magazines and newspapers such as: *We The People*, *The Press Democrat*, the *Bay Area Reporter*, the *Russian River Times*, the *Desert Times*, *In LA Magazine*, and *The Desert Sun*.

Dan has taken his love of nature and his dogs a step further. Now his passion lies with the animal rights movement. His articles on this issue have appeared in *Bay Woof* and *The Dodo* - an online magazine about animals. Dan and his Goldens are well on their way to 20,000 followers on Facebook.